THE PILGRIM'S PROGRESS

DISCIPLESHIP COURSE

A Companion Study to Bunyan's
THE PILGRIM'S PROGRESS
Faithfully Retold

by

Cheryl V. Ford

WESTBOW
PRESS®
A DIVISION OF THOMAS NELSON
& ZONDERVAN

WestBow Press books may be ordered through booksellers or by contacting:

WestBow Press
A Division of Thomas Nelson & Zondervan
1663 Liberty Drive
Bloomington, IN 47403
www.westbowpress.com
1 (866) 928-1240

ISBN: 978-1-5127-5415-5 (sc)
ISBN: 978-1-5127-5414-8 (e)

Print information available on the last page.

WestBow Press rev. date: 10/21/2016

ACKNOWLEDGMENTS . . .

Jesus Christ, of course, receives supreme gratitude and glory. He inspired John Bunyan to pen his magnificent story; He led me to update his work in today's English (*The Pilgrim's Progress,* Tyndale House Publishers); and, He moved me to disciple God's pilgrims through this discipleship course. Thanks to my husband Clay, son Billy, daughter Hannah, and sister Gayle for their encouragement, prayers, support, and help with editing. Billy and Gayle led test study groups through this course and gave invaluable input for perfecting it. Thanks, also, to all my friends who have shown an interest and prayed during this process. Finally, thanks to Westbow Press for their expert work with this volume.

CONTENTS

INTRODUCTION

As I make my slow pilgrimage through the world, a certain sense of beautiful mystery seems to gather and grow.

-- A. C. Benson

Greetings, pilgrim!

Welcome to a unique discipleship experience sure to enrich and deepen your Christian life. One of the greatest and most enduring stories of all time, *The Pilgrim's Progress* has inspired millions for more than 300 years! And now it's your turn!

Before beginning this course . . .

It is most advantageous for you to use Cheryl Ford's version: *The Pilgrim's Progress* (faithfully retold), published by Tyndale House Publishers. Chapters in that book and this course correspond with each other.

Be sure not to skip reading the Preface of *The Pilgrim's Progress*. Providing valuable context to the story, it will tell you about the author, his purpose in writing the story, the impact the story has had on the church and world, and its relevance to our day.

John Bunyan set his story within the context of a Christian pilgrimage. The word *pilgrim* derives from the Latin word *peregrinus*, meaning foreigner. Our English word, peregrine, is a derivation that means foreign, alien, or wandering. In short, therefore, a pilgrimage is the journey of a pilgrim. This word has three distinct meanings in the Bible:

1. Our span of life on earth. Thus, when Jacob met Pharaoh, he described his entire life to that point as his pilgrimage: *And Jacob said to Pharaoh, "The days of the years of my **pilgrimage** are one hundred and thirty years . . . "* (Genesis 47:9 NKJV).
2. The journey of a pilgrim to a sacred place or shrine, especially worshipers of the Lord who traveled to participate in the Jewish feasts in the Temple in Jerusalem: *Blessed are those whose strength is in you, whose hearts are set on **pilgrimage**.* (Psalm 84:5 NIV). (Note this same portion of Scripture in the NASV: *In whose heart are the highways to Zion!*)
3. A long journey or search, especially one of exalted purpose and moral significance. We see it used in the Old Testament in Exodus 6:4 (NKJV): *I have also established My covenant with them, to give them the land of Canaan, the land of their **pilgrimage**, in which they were strangers.* The heroes of faith are described in the New Testament as strangers and pilgrims: *These all died in faith, not having received the promises, but having seen them afar off, and were persuaded of them, and embraced them, and confessed that they were strangers and pilgrims on the earth.* (Hebrews 11:13 KJV). Peter extends this designation to all believers: *Dearly beloved, I beseech you as strangers and pilgrims, to abstain from fleshly lusts, which war against the soul* (1 Peter 2:11 KJV).

God's Word says, *But we are citizens of heaven, where the Lord Jesus Christ lives. . .* (Philippians 3:20 NLT). In view of this fact, two things should be clear to us: This world is not our home, and we are on our way to our true home. As strangers and pilgrims, we cannot sit statically but must keep moving toward our destination. We see it in the story's original title: *The Pilgrim's Progress from This World to That Which Is to Come.*

As you read this amazing story, you will see your own life in the pilgrimage. Each day has eternal significance; each day is a sacred quest; each day brings you nearer to your exalted destiny in God's Kingdom.

The Pilgrim's Progress Discipleship Course is designed both for individuals and groups.

Individuals:
- You can work at your own pace. The primary story in *The Pilgrim's Progress* is divided into 17 chapters. Following this pattern, *The Pilgrim's Progress Discipleship Course* has 17 chapters. After reading the book chapter, do the corresponding chapter's coursework. Perhaps you are one who likes a schedule. You may benefit from the Daily Study Plans section at the end of the book. Here you will find 5-day plans for each of the 17-weeks. You will also find accelerated plans.

Groups:
- A Group Leaders Resource section is included at the back of this book. These resources are provided for an optimal group experience.
- For groups that want an 8, 9 or 13-week group study, rather than a 17-week one, you can go to Daily Study Plans section, also in the back of this book.
- For an even richer group experience, there is a final "celebration week" option provided at the end of the Progressing Together Group Leader's Guide.

Everyone:
- This is a very spiritually enriching course. In order to unpack all the rich treasures, be sure to begin each time in prayer and remain prayerful throughout.
- Be sure to allow adequate time for reflection and forming your answers. We want this to be an enriching time as the Holy Spirit impacts you with clarity, inspiration, and anointing for your pilgrimage. You may even want to use a journal or notebook for recording additional thoughts and inspiration.
- For your convenience, Scripture verses used in each chapter are included at the end of that chapter. This is meant to simplify your study.
- Note, too, that most answers are provided at the end of the book in the Answer Key section. These are merely provided for clarification. For your greatest progress, think through your own answers and then, if needed, refer to the Answers Key.
- Some questions in each chapter are optional. If you want to do less work, you can skip these. They are marked with (*).

> *My sword I give to him that shall succeed me in my pilgrimage, and my courage and skill to him that can get it.*
>
> --John Bunyan

BEFORE YOU COMMENCE THIS PILGRIMAGE

1 Timothy 4:15 urges, "Practice these things, devote yourself to them, so that all may see your progress."

As you begin this study, anticipate progress in your Christian life. Expect God's Spirit to impact and enrich you in significant ways -- sharpening your vision, refining your character, energizing and empowering your faith, strengthening your resolve to follow your King through all the challenges ahead.

As with your life's pilgrimage – which has a beginning and an end -- this course also has a destination. It can be an exciting adventure with a joyful outcome. And that is the goal! Therefore, will you commit at the outset to reach that destination? Will you persevere through this entire course?

It will help with this journey if you write a statement of resolve to refer back to in your weaker moments. Be sure to sign and date it. You can do that here:

_____

_____

_____

_____

_____

_____

_____

_____

_____

_____

_____

_____

_____

_____

On to the pilgrimage!

CHAPTER

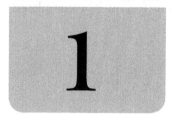

TO BEGIN

Have you ever thought of your Christian life as a pilgrimage? Do you remember a starting point to your pilgrimage? If so, what were some of your thoughts and emotions, both before and after you began?

DRAWN TO THE PILGRIMAGE

1. What is the City of Destruction? What kind of people inhabits this place?

2. What was the burden on the man's back? (See Psalm 38:4 and its context.)

3. What book did he read? How did it influence him? How does Hebrews 4:12 relate to this?

4. (*) The man's family thought he was losing his mind, and he may have thought so, too! Look at Psalm 32:3-5. How did David describe his own experience, and how did he feel once he completed his process of repentance? What does this illustrate for our own lives?

5. Read Psalm 119:71, 75. Can you remember times when you felt deeply convicted, distressed, and even afflicted? Did you come through such times seeing how God used them for good in your life? If not yet, can you entrust your pain to Him and even thank Him for allowing it? Will you do that now? Write a prayer.

~~~~~~~~~~~~~~~~~~~~~~~~~

Progress Memory Verse

Blessed are those whose strength is in you, who have set their hearts on pilgrimage.

--Psalm 84:5 NIV

~~~~~~~~~~~~~~~~~~~~~~~~~

EVANGELIST APPEARS

6. The word "evangelist" comes from two Greek words: *eu* meaning "good" and *angelos* meaning "messenger." Based on this, what do you think an evangelist is, and what was Evangelist's task in the story?

7. Not everyone is called as an evangelist in the Church (see Ephesians 4:11). Yet, every believer should be evangelistic, actively sharing their faith. How is the Holy Spirit encouraging you to be more evangelistic?

PURSUED BY OBSTINATE AND PLIABLE

8. After Evangelist shared which way to go—directing the man to focus on the Light until he comes to a gate—the man fled his family.

   a. Why did he feel this need?

   b. How might Matthew 10:32-39 apply to his decision?

9. (*) How do you think we should respond to those who would discourage or divert us from our pilgrimage?

~~~~~~~~~~~~~~~~~~~~~~~~~

A Note of Encouragement

Eventually, the man's family found their way out of the City of Destruction and embarked on their own pilgrimages. Their story is found in Part 2 of *The Pilgrim's Progress*.

~~~~~~~~~~~~~~~~~~~~~~~~~

10. The Bible claims, "Rebellion is as sinful as witchcraft, and stubbornness as bad as worshiping idols" (1 Samuel 15:23, NLT). Which character represents stubborn people in the story? How did he seek to get the man (now identified as "Christian") and his friend to turn back?

11. In Matthew 13:44, Jesus compares His kingdom to a treasure for which one sells all to obtain. Obstinate believes otherwise. He thinks it's crazy to abandon the world system for a pilgrimage and tries to discourage Christian from doing so. Have you had Obstinates in your own experience? What do you think is the best way to respond to them?

12. How is Pliable presented in this story? What was missing in Pliable's experience that Christian had to endure?

13. "Pliable" means "easily bent, shaped, influenced, swayed." A pliable person is one who is flexible, changeable, and adaptable (the opposite of Obstinate). How do you think this trait might be beneficial, and how might it be detrimental?

14. Forsaking the world can be costly. Have you found it so? Obstinate and Pliable represent human vulnerabilities. Think about your particular vulnerabilities. What are they, and what can you do right now to get past them and live a more victorious pilgrimage?

CHRISTIAN AND PLIABLE DISCUSS HEAVENLY THINGS

15. The glories of heaven are beyond our wildest imagination. Christian exulted in what he foresaw at the end of his pilgrimage. These things dazzled Pliable, too. What about Christian's description most excites you and helps motivate you in your pilgrimage?

THE SLOUGH OF DESPOND AND HELP

16. The Slough of Despond presented Christian and Pliable with a watershed moment in their young faith. Both wrestled to get through the trial but with different outcomes. What made the difference?

17. In your opinion, what kind of things might cause someone to begin a pilgrimage with great enthusiasm but then abort it just as quickly?

18. Help describes good and substantial steps to help pilgrims avoid landing in the Slough. Why did Christian say he missed the steps?

19. What are the steps in the Slough of Despond? (Hint: Bunyan gives this answer in the story's sidebar.) How can the steps help us? (See 2 Peter 1:3-4.)

20. What does 2 Corinthians 1:20 assure us about these steps?

~~~~~~~~~~~~~~~~~~~~~~~~

Key Pilgrim's Perspective

God's Word is the pilgrim's book. It speaks the truth, convicts of sin, changes the heart, renews the spirit, fills us with hope, and guides the way. We can have confidence in the Word. God keeps His promises. He never made one that was too good to be true.

~~~~~~~~~~~~~~~~~~~~~~~~

21. Have you ever experienced a trial similar to the Slough of Despond? What help did God send you?

22. Can you think of some favorite Bible promises that act as steps to help keep you steady? Write down a few.

NOTES:

SCRIPTURES USED IN THIS CHAPTER

Psalm 38:1-5

O LORD, rebuke me not in your anger, nor discipline me in your wrath! ²For your arrows have sunk into me, and your hand has come down on me. ³There is no soundness in my flesh because of your indignation; there is no health in my bones because of my sin.⁴For my iniquities have gone over my head; like a heavy burden, they are too heavy for me.⁵My wounds stink and fester because of my foolishness.

Hebrews 4:12

For the word of God is living and active, sharper than any two-edged sword, piercing to the division of soul and of spirit, of joints and of marrow, and discerning the thoughts and intentions of the heart.

Psalm 32:3-5

For when I kept silent, my bones wasted away through my groaning all day long. ⁴For day and night your hand was heavy upon me; my strength was dried up as by the heat of summer. Selah
⁵I acknowledged my sin to you, and I did not cover my iniquity; I said, "I will confess my transgressions to the LORD," and you forgave the iniquity of my sin. Selah

Psalm 119:71, 75

⁷¹It is good for me that I was afflicted, that I might learn your statutes.⁷⁵I know, O LORD, that your rules are righteous, and that in faithfulness you have afflicted me.

Ephesians 4:11 NLT

Now these are the gifts Christ gave to the church: the apostles, the prophets, the evangelists, and the pastors and teachers.

Matthew 10:32-39

So everyone who acknowledges me before men, I also will acknowledge before my Father who is in heaven, ³³but whoever denies me before men, I also will deny before my Father who is in heaven. ³⁴"Do not think that I have come to bring peace to the earth. I have not come to bring peace, but a sword. ³⁵For I have come to set a man against his father, and a daughter against her mother, and a daughter-in-law against her mother-in-law. ³⁶And a person's enemies will be those of his own household. ³⁷Whoever loves father or mother more than me is not worthy of me, and whoever loves son or daughter more than me is not worthy of me. ³⁸And whoever does not take his cross and follow me is not worthy of me. ³⁹Whoever finds his life will lose it, and whoever loses his life for my sake will find it.

Matthew 13:44

The kingdom of heaven is like treasure hidden in a field, which a man found and covered up. Then in his joy he goes and sells all that he has and buys that field.

2 Peter 1:3-4

His divine power has granted to us all things that pertain to life and godliness, through the knowledge of him who called us to his own glory and excellence, ⁴by which he has granted to us his precious and very great promises, so that through them you may become partakers of the divine nature, having escaped from the corruption that is in the world because of sinful desire.

2 Corinthians 1:20 NLT

That whatever promises God has made in Scripture, Christ fulfilled them all. Each is reliable, and we can stand on them. When we say, "Amen," we say it confidently, and to God's glory.

CHAPTER

2

TO BEGIN

Have you ever gotten into a mess by ignoring good advice? What lesson, if any, did you learn from that experience?

CHRISTIAN MEETS WORLDLY-WISEMAN

1. Worldly-wiseman was from a city named Carnal Policy. What would be the guiding principle of such a place?

~~~~~~

Definition: Carnal

The word "carnal" comes from the Greek *sarkikos*, which derives from *sarx*, meaning "flesh." The King James Version uses "carnal" ten times in the New Testament. Romans 8:7, for instance, speaks of the carnal mind, saying it is at enmity with God. Other versions translate the word *sarkikos* to "flesh" or "sinful mind." The word "carnal," therefore, denotes being governed by the lower, earthly nature (the sensual animal appetites) rather than by God's Spirit. This earthly nature is prone to sin and is opposed to God. A worldly person is a carnal one.

~~~~~~~~~~~~~~~~~~~~~~~~~~~~~~~~~~~

2. A false-prophet is one who teaches false doctrine and leads people away from the true Gospel and biblical teachings. What does the Apostle Paul say concerning them in Galatians 1:8?

3. In Acts 20:29-31, what does Paul sternly warn us against, and what action does he say to take?

4. Still under the burden of his sin, Christian wants peace. Worldly-wiseman offers him speedy relief, but it's not God's peace. What are some ways the world lures people today into a false sense of peace and well-being?

5. What does the village of Morality represent? What about Legality and his son Civility?

~~~~~~~~~~~~~~~~~~~~~~~~~~~~~

Progress Memory Verse

Be careful that you don't let anyone rob you through his philosophy and vain deceit, after the tradition of men, after the elements of the world, and not after Christ.

-- Colossians 2:8

~~~~~~~~~~~~~~~~~~~~~~~~~~~~~

6. Carnality directs Worldly-wiseman's thinking. What else do we know about his belief system and view of salvation?

7. How do you think Worldy-wiseman's religious persuasion negates the need for God's grace?

8. What was the consequence of Christian heeding Worldly-wiseman's advice?

9. According to Isaiah 64:6, why do our best efforts to establish our own righteousness fall short?

10. Of course, the worldly-wise hold many views that oppose the Gospel. Think about your own vulnerability. Ask the Holy Spirit to help you detect any ways the worldly-wise influence you by their carnal reasoning. How do you think you can better guard against their undermining of God's truth?

EVANGELIST DELIVERS CHRISTIAN FROM ERROR

11. Why was the reunion between Christian and Evangelist a difficult one?

12. Christian already felt bad. Why plow into him with hard Scriptures? Do you think Evangelist should have been kinder? Explain.

13. (*) Read Hebrews 13:7. What is your response to this? If a more mature Christian corrects you, how do you generally receive it? Can you think of any way you can do better?

14. What three things does Evangelist warn Christian to abhor concerning Worldly-wiseman's counsel? What in his lecture most resonates with you?

    a.

    b.

    c.

15. Evangelist holds to the narrow view that there is only one legitimate way for Christian to go. That way does not include a detour to Mt. Sinai. Why do you think this is a critical point? (See Acts 4:12 and Galatians 3:10-11.)

16. (*) What do you think makes the counsel of the worldly-wise appealing?

17. Pretend you are Christian and you just read Matthew 7:13-14 in the book you carry. Upon hearing Worldly-wiseman's advice, what would you say to him and to those he seeks to deceive? According to this passage, why was Christian walking the road to life alone? Why might you need to do this at times?

CHRISTIAN IS FORGIVEN

18. What good news did Evangelist give to Christian?

19. Unfortunately, there are worldly-wise people in positions of influence throughout our culture. These religious humanists do great damage to those with fledgling faith. On the other hand, there are those who unflinchingly proclaim the Gospel truth. Can you name some heroes whom you admire, who faithfully deliver the Good News?

~~~~~~~~~~~~~~~~~~~~~~~~~~

Scriptures for Further Reflection

Exodus 19:10-22
Isaiah 29:14
James 4:7-10
1 Corinthians 2:2-5
2 Corinthians 3:4-6
Hebrews 2:1-3

~~~~~~~~~~~~~~~~~~~~~~~~

NOTES:

_____

_____

_____

_____

_____

_____

_____

_____

_____

_____

_____

_____

_____

_____

_____

_____

_____

_____

_____

_____

_____

_____

SCRIPTURES USED IN THIS CHAPTER

Galatians 1:8
But even if we or an angel from heaven should preach to you a gospel contrary to the one we preached to you, let him be accursed.

Acts 20:29-31
I know that after my departure fierce wolves will come in among you, not sparing the flock; [30]and from among your own selves will arise men speaking twisted things, to draw away the disciples after them. [31]Therefore be alert, remembering that for three years I did not cease night or day to admonish everyone with tears.

Isaiah 64:6
We have all become like one who is unclean, and all our righteous deeds are like a polluted garment. We all fade like a leaf, and our iniquities, like the wind, take us away.

Hebrews 13:7
Remember your leaders, those who spoke to you the word of God. Consider the outcome of their way of life, and imitate their faith.

Acts 4:12
And there is salvation in no one else, for there is no other name under heaven given among men by which we must be saved.

Galatians 3:10-11
For all who rely on works of the law are under a curse; for it is written, "Cursed be everyone who does not abide by all things written in the Book of the Law, and do them."[11]Now it is evident that no one is justified before God by the law, for "The righteous shall live by faith."

Matthew 7:13-14
Enter by the narrow gate. For the gate is wide and the way is easy that leads to destruction, and those who enter by it are many. [14]For the gate is narrow and the way is hard that leads to life, and those who find it are few.

2 Timothy 4:3-4
For the time is coming when people will not endure sound teaching, but having itching ears they will accumulate for themselves teachers to suit their own passions, [4]and will turn away from listening to the truth and wander off into myths.

CHAPTER

3

~~~~~~~~~~~~~~~~~~~~~~~~

Progress Memory Verse

Teach me to do your will, for you are my God. Your Spirit is good. Lead me in the land of uprightness.

--Psalm 143:10

~~~~~~~~~~~~~~~~~~~~~~~~

TO BEGIN

Has the Holy Spirit ever given you a special dream, vision, or insight? Describe it and record what it meant to you:

CHRISTIAN MEETS GOOD-WILL AND ENTERS THE GATE

1. The Wicket Gate is a small gate. Why do you think Bunyan chose a small gate as the next and vital step on this pilgrimage? (See Matthew 7:13-14 again.)

2. Why would Beelzebub (another name for the devil) choose this particular place to kill pilgrims?

~~~~~~~~~~~~~~~~~~~~~~

Definition: Wicket Gate

A wicket gate, or simply a wicket, is a small and narrow door or gate typically built into a larger door, a castle wall, a city gate, or a fence. The larger, heavier gate is designed for the passage of wagons or other vehicles. The wicket gate, on the other hand, is only one-person wide and designed to let individuals through when the large gate is closed. In this way, guards can better control access.

~~~~~~~~~~~~~~~~~~~~~~

3. How does Good-will represent God's love?

~~~~~~~~~~~~~~~~~~~~~~~~

Progress Tip

Beautiful and comforting words are found above the little Wicket Gate: "Knock and the door will be opened to you" (Matthew 7:7). Only sincere pilgrims come this way, and they must come humbly. This gate is wide enough to let us through with our burden of sin but not wide enough to permit us to come through with our pride intact. Don't try to take your stubborn pride through Christ's gate; it will only thwart your progress.

~~~~~~~~~~~~~~~~~~~~~~~~

THE INTERPRETER'S HOUSE

4. The Interpreter represents the Holy Spirit. Why does this name suit Him, and why is this significant? (See John 14:26 and 1 Corinthians 2:12-13.)

5. Have you ever asked the Holy Spirit for more revelation but felt like you were left outside knocking? Read Luke 11:9-13. What encouragement do you find in this passage?

THE MAN IN THE PICTURE

6. Who is the "man in the picture," and what does his portrayal represent? What is his authority? (See Hebrews 13:17.)

7. Why is it important for us to study the "man in the picture"?

8. What are the six characteristics of a true minister according to this portrait? Briefly explain what you think they mean:

   a.

   b.

   c.

   d.

   e.

   f.

THE ROOM FILLED WITH DUST

9. What biblical truth do you see conveyed by "the room filled with dust"?

PASSION AND PATIENCE

10. What do Passion and Patience represent?

11. (*) In our culture, so many are like Passion. How do you see this malady infecting the church? Can you think of people you admire who are more like Patience?

12. Think about your own struggles between Passion and Patience. How can you weaken the Passion syndrome, and how can you strengthen the Patience virtue?

THE FIRE BY THE WALL

13. How does the story of the "fire burning against the wall" encourage believers?

THE BEAUTIFUL (STATELY) PALACE

14. Christian sees a stately palace. We see many people who want to enter but only one who actually does so. What made the difference?

~~~~~~

Key Pilgrim's Perspective #1: A Stately Palace

In case the pilgrim thinks the lesson of Patience means passivity, the Interpreter reveals a "Stately Palace" where only one person has the courageous faith to enter. This one exemplifies the tenacious determination it takes to fight through stubborn and even fierce resistance to participate in God's Kingdom. He will not let himself be denied.

Because the world, the flesh, and the devil conspire against our becoming Jesus' disciples, it takes bold resoluteness to overcome them. Similar to the Israelites who had a Promised Land to possess, we must engage in a fight of faith to receive the benefits of the Kingdom. While salvation is a free gift, it must be possessed. *The one who conquers, I will grant him to sit with me on my throne, as I also conquered and sat down with my Father on his throne* (Revelation 3:21).

~~~~~~

15. Pursuing the true Gospel can be dangerous. Reflecting on the Stately Palace, are you prepared to face suffering, opposition, and difficulties that come with entering God's Kingdom? How did Paul and Barnabus advise believers about this? (See Acts 14:21-22.)

16. What does the story of the "stately palace" tell us about passive faith vs. active faith?

THE MAN IN THE IRON CAGE

17. What does the "man in the iron cage" convey?

18. (*) How do Galatians 6:1 and 2 Timothy 2:24-26 instruct us to approach people who need repentance?

~~~~~~

Key Pilgrim's Perspective #2: The Man in the Iron Cage

Christian is shown this tragic man to impress upon him the importance of staying cautiously watchful. This man, by his own admission, has grieved the Holy Spirit and fallen away from God. While The Interpreter never says his situation is hopeless, the man believes it is. As Bunyan notes in his sidebar, "Despair is as an iron cage." Sometimes people languish in fear of eternal separation when they have every reason for hope. And there is reason for hope in this man's case: 1. He shows concern for his spiritual condition. 2. He has no pleasure in his former sin. 3. He is not yet in Hell. Here he sits, however, locked in a cage of unbelief and despair due to his sin. The Interpreter does not address the issue of this man's ultimate destination. He wants, instead, to impress upon Christian that willful sin is exceedingly dangerous and leads to utter bondage.

~~~~~~

19. What do you think of the warnings presented by "the man in the iron cage"? If there is peril to indulging in sinful thoughts and behavior, will you resolve to confess and repent of them quickly?

THE MAN WITH THE TERRIFYING DREAM

20. Consider "the man with the terrifying dream." What if Christ returns tomorrow? Are you prepared to meet Him? Keeping this story in mind and also 2 Peter 3:9-14, how do you intend to live?

~~~~~~~~~~~~~~~~~~~~~~~~~~~~

Progress Quote from Another Pilgrim

In any matter where we have questions, we have a right to ask the Holy Spirit to lead us and to expect His gentle guiding.

-- Curtis Hutson

~~~~~~~~~~~~~~~~~~~~~~~~~~~~

21. The Interpreter taught Christian a variety of important lessons: some hopeful and some troubling. Which spoke most to your life? In the coming weeks, what can you do to apply these lessons?

~~~~~~~~~~~~~~~~~~~~~~~~

Scriptures for Further Reflection

Isaiah 30:18-19
John 14:16-17; 15:26; 16:12-15
Matthew 11:12
1 Thessalonians 5:6-9
Hebrews 6:4-6
Matthew 24:26-31
Revelation 20:11-15

~~~~~~~~~~~~~~~~~~~~~~~~

NOTES:

_____

_____

_____

_____

_____

_____

_____

_____

_____

_____

_____

_____

_____

_____

_____

_____

_____

SCRIPTURES USED IN THIS CHAPTER

Matthew 7:13-14
Enter by the narrow gate. For the gate is wide and the way is easy that leads to destruction, and those who enter by it are many. [14]For the gate is narrow and the way is hard that leads to life, and those who find it are few.

John 14:26
But the Helper, the Holy Spirit, whom the Father will send in my name, he will teach you all things and bring to your remembrance all that I have said to you.

1 Corinthians 2:12-13
Now we have received not the spirit of the world, but the Spirit who is from God, that we might understand the things freely given us by God. [13]And we impart this in words not taught by human wisdom but taught by the Spirit, interpreting spiritual truths to those who are spiritual.

Luke 11:9-13 NLT
"And so I tell you, keep on asking, and you will receive what you ask for. Keep on seeking, and you will find. Keep on knocking, and the door will be opened to you. [10]For everyone who asks, receives. Everyone who seeks, finds. And to everyone who knocks, the door will be opened. [11]"You fathers — if your children ask for a fish, do you give them a snake instead? [12]Or if they ask for an egg, do you give them a scorpion? Of course not! [13]So if you sinful people know how to give good gifts to your children, how much more will your heavenly Father give the Holy Spirit to those who ask him."

Hebrews 13:17
Obey your leaders and submit to them, for they are keeping watch over your souls, as those who will have to give an account. Let them do this with joy and not with groaning, for that would be of no advantage to you.

Acts 14:21-22
When they had preached the gospel to that city and had made many disciples, they returned to Lystra and to Iconium and to Antioch, [22]strengthening the souls of the disciples, encouraging them to continue in the faith, and saying that through many tribulations we must enter the kingdom of God.

Galatians 6:1
Brothers, if anyone is caught in any transgression, you who are spiritual should restore him in a spirit of gentleness. Keep watch on yourself, lest you too be tempted.

2 Timothy 2:24-26 WEB
The Lord's servant must not quarrel, but be gentle towards all, able to teach, patient, [25]in gentleness correcting those who oppose him: perhaps God may give them repentance leading to a full knowledge of the truth, [26]and they may recover themselves out of the devil's snare, having been taken captive by him to his will.

2 Peter 3:9-14
The Lord is not slow to fulfill his promise as some count slowness, but is patient toward you, not wishing that any should perish, but that all should reach repentance. [10]ut the day of the Lord will come like a thief, and then the heavens will pass away with a roar, and the heavenly bodies will be burned up and dissolved, and the earth and the works that are done on it will be exposed. [11]Since all these things are thus to be dissolved, what sort of people ought you to be in lives of holiness and godliness, [12]waiting for and hastening the coming of the day of God, because of which the heavens will be set on fire and dissolved, and the heavenly bodies will melt as they burn! [13]But according to his promise we are waiting for new heavens and a new earth in which righteousness dwells. [14]Therefore, beloved, since you are waiting for these, be diligent to be found by him without spot or blemish, and at peace.

CHAPTER

Progress Memory Verse

For the word of the cross is folly to those who are perishing, but to us who are being saved it is the power of God.

-- 1 Corinthians 1:18

~~~~~~~~~~~~~~~~~~~~~~~~~

TO BEGIN

Think about your story. How long have you been a believer? How did you lose your burden of sin? What have you loved most about your pilgrimage thus far?

CHRISTIAN REACHES THE CROSS

1. Christian finally lost his burden! How and why did this happen, and where did it go?

2. Why do you think Christian's burden disappeared into a grave?

3. Christian stopped and stood in awe of the Cross and what it had done for him. Have you stopped and gazed at the wonderful Cross lately? Have you recently experienced the joy of being freed from your burden? Take a few moments to reflect upon all that the Cross means to you. Record some of your thoughts and feelings here.

4. Three Shining Ones give Christian gifts to further confirm that he is now a child of God. Who are these three, and what are their gifts?

5.   A Shining One gave Christian new garments. How do Zechariah 3:3-4, Isaiah 61:10, and Luke 15:22 relate to this?

6.   What is the seal God has given believers, and what does it do? (See Ephesians 1:13-14.)

FALSE CHRISTIANS ALONG THE WAY

7.   Christian meets three sleeping characters on the way. Who are they; what are their individual flaws; and what do they hold in common?

8.   (*) In Matthew 26:31-45, Peter makes a critical error. What was it? How was his error like that of Simple, Sloth, and Presumption? What was the result?

9.   In Matthew 24:4, 42; 25:13; 26:38, 41, we find Jesus warning His disciples (including Peter) repeatedly. What was His warning, and why did He give it?

~~~~~~

Definition: Watchfulness

Watchfulness is a state of staying observant, alert, and vigilant. A watchman is one whose duty it is to keep a vigil. Often, watchmen guard their city from walls, especially at night.

The theme of keeping watch is seen repeatedly in the Bible. In the Old Testament, Ezekiel is called as a spiritual watchman (33:7). In the New Testament, believers are urged to stay watchful.

Watchfulness involves a number of things. We watch for deceivers -- *Watch out that no-one deceives you* (Mark 13:5, NIV). We watch against sin and carelessness in our own lives − *Watch your life and doctrine closely* (1 Timothy. 4:16, NIV). We watch for the Second Coming of Christ -- *Watch therefore, for you know neither the day nor the hour* (Matthew 25:13). And Jesus tethers it to prayer in His command -- "Watch and pray" (Matthew 26:41).

Genuine spiritual health manifests in vigilant watchfulness. This keeps the Church faithful in dark and perilous times.

~~~~~~

10. (*) Can you think of specific things you can do to avoid the failure of Simple, Sloth, Presumption . . . and Peter?

11. How did Formality and Hypocrisy differ from Christian?

12. What kind of religious people do you think Formality and Hypocrisy represent? Do you think there are many like them in churches today?

13. Many people want to go to heaven but ignore the "Master's Rule." Why is the Master's Rule important, especially today? How do John 10:7-9 and Matthew 7:21-23 serve as warnings to people like Formality and Hypocrisy?

Progress Quote from Another Pilgrim

I walk firmer and more secure uphill than down.

--Michel de Montaigne

THREE WAYS FROM WHICH TO CHOOSE

14. Christian, Formality, and Hypocrisy come to a Hill where we see three divergent paths. What are they, and why is the correct path so difficult?

15. What does the Hill Difficulty mean to you, personally? What have been some of the most difficult experiences you have had as a Christian? How did you get through them?

Key Pilgrim's Perspective

As we look upon our own Hill Difficulty, it may seem steep and high; we may want an easier route. But this is the only true way, and there is no sliding up this hill. It requires a climb.

Those who look for an easy way recoil at the difficulty they see in their opportunity. Obedient and faith-filled pilgrims, on the other hand, find inspiration in the opportunity they see in their difficulty.

We should not give up when God's way gets hard. Rather than taking an easier way, we should resolve to go forward. Difficulty can be a great gift in life. Our difficult challenges provide invaluable opportunities for personal growth by which we may fulfill our deepest dreams and truest purposes in life. It's good to remember that our faithful God is always there with us in our difficulty.

CHRISTIAN LOSES HIS SCROLL AT THE PLEASANT ARBOR

16. What might the Pleasant Arbor represent?

RESPONDING TO FEAR

17. When the two cowards Timorous and Mistrust came running down the hill, Christian wondered if he should keep going. Have you ever met people or situations that left you fearful and doubting that the Lord was really with you? What does 1 Corinthians 10:13 promise, and how can you use it on your pilgrimage?

RECOVERING THE SCROLL

18. Christian lost his scroll on Hill Difficulty. What caused this loss of assurance, and how did this lead to more grief? What turned this situation around?

FACING LIONS IN THE WAY

19. If the stately palace named Beautiful represents church fellowship, what might the lions represent? How did Christian overcome his fear of them?

~~~~~~

Progress Quote from Another Pilgrim

Unbelief generally has a good eye for the lions, but a blind eye for the chains that hold them back. It is quite true that there are difficulties in the way of those who profess to be followers of the Lord Jesus Christ. We do not desire to conceal this fact, and we do not wish you to come amongst us without counting the cost. But it is also true that these difficulties have a limit which they cannot pass. Like the lions in the pilgrim's pathway, they are chained, and restrained, and absolutely under the control of the Lord God Almighty.

--Charles H. Spurgeon

~~~~~~

20. Do you have lions that roar at you? The Apostle Paul suffered many trials and serious opposition yet fulfilled his destiny. Read his declaration in Philippians 3:8-14. What are some key points that you find helpful?

~~~~~~~~~~~~~~~~~~~~~~~~~~

Scriptures for Further Reflection

Ephesians 5:14-17
John 3:3-6
Proverbs 14:12
Hebrews 10:22-23
1 Thessalonians 5:7-8
2 Timothy 4:17-18

~~~~~~~~~~~~~~~~~~~~~~~~~~

NOTES:

_____

_____

_____

_____

_____

_____

_____

_____

_____

_____

_____

_____

_____

_____

_____

_____

_____

_____

_____

_____

_____

SCRIPTURES USED IN THIS CHAPTER

Zechariah 3:3-4 WEB

Now Joshua was clothed with filthy garments, and was standing before the angel. [4]He answered and spoke to those who stood before him, saying, "Take the filthy garments off him." To him he said, "Behold, I have caused your iniquity to pass from you, and I will clothe you with rich clothing."

Isaiah 61:10

I will greatly rejoice in the LORD; my soul shall exult in my God, for he has clothed me with the garments of salvation; he has covered me with the robe of righteousness, as a bridegroom decks himself like a priest with a beautiful headdress, and as a bride adorns herself with her jewels.

Luke 15:22

But the father said to his servants, 'Bring quickly the best robe, and put it on him, and put a ring on his hand, and shoes on his feet.

Ephesians 1:13-14

In him you also, when you heard the word of truth, the gospel of your salvation, and believed in him, were sealed with the promised Holy Spirit, [14]who is the guarantee of our inheritance until we acquire possession of it, to the praise of his glory.

Matthew 26:31-45

Then Jesus said to them, "You will all fall away because of me this night. For it is written, 'I will strike the shepherd, and the sheep of the flock will be scattered.' [32]But after I am raised up, I will go before you to Galilee." [33]Peter answered him, "Though they all fall away because of you, I will never fall away." [34]Jesus said to him, "Truly, I tell you, this very night, before the rooster crows, you will deny me three times." [35]Peter said to him, "Even if I must die with you, I will not deny you!" And all the disciples said the same. [36]Then Jesus went with them to a place called Gethsemane, and he said to his disciples, "Sit here, while I go over there and pray." [37]And taking with him Peter and the two sons of Zebedee, he began to be sorrowful and troubled. [38]Then he said to them, "My soul is very sorrowful, even to death; remain here, and watch with me." [39]And going a little farther he fell on his face and prayed, saying, "My Father, if it be possible, let this cup pass from me; nevertheless, not as I will, but as you will." [40]And he came to the disciples and found them sleeping. And he said to Peter, "So, could you not watch with me one hour? [41]Watch and pray that you may not enter into temptation. The spirit indeed is willing, but the flesh is weak." [42]Again, for the second time, he went away and prayed, "My Father, if this cannot pass unless I drink it, your will be done." [43]And again he came and found them sleeping, for their eyes were heavy. [44]So, leaving them again, he went away and prayed for the third time, saying the same words again. [45]Then he came to the disciples and said to them, "Sleep and take your rest later on. See, the hour is at hand, and the Son of Man is betrayed into the hands of sinners.

Matthew 24:4, 42; 25:13; 26:38, 41

And Jesus answered them, "See that no one leads you astray. . . [42]Therefore, stay awake, for you do not know on what day your Lord is coming. . . [13]Watch therefore, for you know neither the day nor the hour. . . [38]Then he said to them, "My soul is very sorrowful, even to death; remain here, and watch with me" . . . [41]Watch and pray that you may not enter into temptation. The spirit indeed is willing, but the flesh is weak."

John 10:7-9

So Jesus again said to them, "Truly, truly, I say to you, I am the door of the sheep. [8]All who came before me are thieves and robbers, but the sheep did not listen to them. [9]I am the door. If anyone enters by me, he will be saved and will go in and out and find pasture.

Matthew 7:21-23

"Not everyone who says to me, 'Lord, Lord,' will enter the kingdom of heaven, but the one who does the will of my Father who is in heaven. [22]On that day many will say to me, 'Lord, Lord, did we not prophesy in your name, and cast out demons in your name, and do many mighty works in your name?' [23]And then will I declare to them, 'I never knew you; depart from me, you workers of lawlessness.'

1 Corinthians 10:13

No temptation has overtaken you that is not common to man. God is faithful, and he will not let you be tempted beyond your ability, but with the temptation he will also provide the way of escape, that you may be able to endure it.

Philippians 3:8-14 NLT

Yes, everything else is worthless when compared with the infinite value of knowing Christ Jesus my Lord. For his sake I have discarded everything else, counting it all as garbage, so that I could gain Christ [9]and become one with him. I no longer count on my own righteousness through obeying the law; rather, I become righteous through faith in Christ. For God's way of making us right with himself depends on faith. [10]I want to know Christ and experience the mighty power that raised him from the dead. I want to suffer with him, sharing in his death, [11]so that one way or another I will experience the resurrection from the dead! [12]I don't mean to say that I have already achieved these things or that I have already reached perfection. But I press on to possess that perfection for which Christ Jesus first possessed me. [13]No, dear brothers and sisters, I have not achieved it, but I focus on this one thing: Forgetting the past and looking forward to what lies ahead, [14]I press on to reach the end of the race and receive the heavenly prize for which God, through Christ Jesus, is calling us.

CHAPTER

TO BEGIN

What does Christian fellowship mean to you? Can you think of any particularly meaningful times you've had with other believers? Explain.

RECEIVED AT THE PALACE BEAUTIFUL

1. The Palace Beautiful represents church fellowship. Who, therefore, would the gatekeeper Watchful represent? Why would he screen Christian before admitting him into the Palace?

2. Before gaining admittance to the Palace, Christian is interviewed by Discretion. Today, the word *discretion* has more to do with the ability to make good judgments related to one's own actions. In Bunyan's time, discretion meant discernment. With so much spiritual confusion and falsehood today, why is discretion important to the church? (See Matthew 7:15 and Acts 20:28-31.)

~~~~~~~~~~~~~~~~~~~~~~

Progress Memory Verse

Let's consider how to provoke one another to love and good works, not forsaking our own assembling together, as the custom of some is, but exhorting one another, and so much the more, as you see the Day approaching.

--Hebrews 10:25

~~~~~~~~~~~~~~~~~~~~~~

3. The members of the Palace welcomed Christian in, saying, "Come in, man blessed of the Lord." Think about your particular fellowship. Do you think of yourself as blessed to be part of this church family? What are some strengths you see in your fellowship, and how can you do more to enrich and deepen it so everyone feels blessed to participate?

4. Christian meets Discretion, Prudence, Piety, and Charity. What do these names mean, and how do they represent important qualities of healthy church life? (Use a dictionary, if needed.)

   Discretion:

   Prudence:

   Piety:

   Charity:

5. How is true fellowship expressed in the Palace? Why is our definition and experience of fellowship sometimes weak?

~~~~~~~~~~~~~~~~~~~~~~~~~

Definition: Fellowship

This word in the Greek is Koinonia (*Κοινωνια*). Rich in meaning, it indicates the communion (or common faith) of Christians. It is their shared life, which includes experiences, expressions of faith, partnership, and relationship with God.

~~~~~~~~~~~~~~~~~~~~~~~~~

6. If the meal together represents the Lord's Supper, what makes this portrayal noteworthy?

THE ROOM CALLED PEACE

7. Why would an experience of peace follow the events of this day?

8. Do you think the room called Peace represents peace *with* God or the peace *of* God? Is there a difference? In view of Christian's prior experiences on Hill Difficulty, why was this experience important?

9. Do you have fears, anxieties, guilt, or stresses that hinder your ability to enjoy God's peace? What can you do to overcome these things?

~~~~~~

Key Pilgrim's Perspective

Christ first calls us into fellowship with Himself and then with each other. In Scripture, we see a dramatic intertwining of these relationships: *God is to be trusted, the God who called you to have fellowship with his Son Jesus Christ, our Lord.[10] By the authority of our Lord Jesus Christ I appeal to all of you, my friends, to agree in what you say, so that there will be no divisions among you. Be completely united, with only one thought and one purpose* (1 Corinthians 1:9-10, GNT). *If we say we have fellowship with him while we walk in darkness, we lie and do not practice the truth. But if we walk in the light, as he is in the light, we have fellowship with one another, and the blood of Jesus his Son cleanses us from all sin* (1 John 1:6-7).

Christ died for individuals, but He also died to form a people who live in fellowship with Him and with each other. When our fellowship deepens, we enjoy increased intimacy with Him and each other – what Paul calls the "fellowship of the Holy Spirit" (2 Corinthians 13:14).

We are strangers and pilgrims passing through hostile territory in this world. Recognizing this truth makes our common bond all the more precious. Truly, we *need* each other; and that means we need fellowship.

~~~~~~

THE STUDY AND THE ARMORY

10. What does the visit to the Study represent? Why do you think it took place early in the day?

11. Read 2 Timothy 2:15. Do most Christians today take Bible study seriously enough? What is the price of our complacency?

12. (*) Do you visit the Study with other believers often enough? Does it generate boredom or enthusiasm in you? What can you do to make your experience more spiritually edifying?

13. Of what significance is the Armory, and how does Ephesians 6:10-18 apply?

~~~~~~~~~~~~~~~~~~~~~~~~

Progress Tip

Because our own armor would be worthless in spiritual combat, God's Word commands us to put on the armor that God provides: "the full armor of God." But God does not expect us to do this alone. Just as we see Christian's friends equipping him with the armor, we help each other with it. Our culture tends to think individualistically. But we become most effective as we team up, learning to love, trust, and rely on the Spirit's enablement together.

~~~~~~~~~~~~~~~~~~~~~~~~

14. Why would a lovely Palace with rooms for fellowship, peace, and study also boast a place indicative of conflict and war? Does a young Christian really need an "Armory"?

15. What do the various instruments used by heroes tell us about how God equips His people for doing great things?

THE DELECTABLE MOUNTAINS AND RESUMING THE JOURNEY

16. What do you think the Delectable Mountains represent? Why do you think they are important to observe?

17. The young pilgrim must go down into the Valley of Humiliation. What do you think that represents? For a clue, read 2 Corinthians 12:1-10.

18. Bunyan placed the Palace Beautiful early in the pilgrimage. What truth do you think he was trying to convey?

~~~~~~~~~~~~~~~~~~~~~~~~

Scriptures for Further Reflection

Acts 2:42-47
1 Thessalonians 5:11
Proverbs 2:11-15
1 John 1:3
Luke 22:19-20
Philippians 4:6-7
Hebrews 11:32-34
1 Peter 5:5-6

~~~~~~~~~~~~~~~~~~~~~~~~

NOTES:

_____

_____

_____

_____

_____

_____

_____

_____

_____

_____

_____

_____

_____

_____

_____

_____

_____

_____

_____

_____

SCRIPTURES USED IN THIS CHAPTER

Matthew. 7:15
Beware of false prophets, who come to you in sheep's clothing but inwardly are ravenous wolves.

Acts 20:28-31
Pay careful attention to yourselves and to all the flock, in which the Holy Spirit has made you overseers, to care for the church of God, which he obtained with his own blood. [29]I know that after my departure fierce wolves will come in among you, not sparing the flock; [30]and from among your own selves will arise men speaking twisted things, to draw away the disciples after them. [31]Therefore be alert, remembering that for three years I did not cease night or day to admonish everyone with tears.

2 Timothy 2:15
Do your best to present yourself to God as one approved, a worker who has no need to be ashamed, rightly handling the word of truth.

Ephesians 6:10-18

Finally, be strong in the Lord and in the strength of his might. [11]Put on the whole armor of God, that you may be able to stand against the schemes of the devil. [12]For we do not wrestle against flesh and blood, but against the rulers, against the authorities, against the cosmic powers over this present darkness, against the spiritual forces of evil in the heavenly places. [13]Therefore take up the whole armor of God, that you may be able to withstand in the evil day, and having done all, to stand firm. [14]Stand therefore, having fastened on the belt of truth, and having put on the breastplate of righteousness, [15]and, as shoes for your feet, having put on the readiness given by the gospel of peace. [16]In all circumstances take up the shield of faith, with which you can extinguish all the flaming darts of the evil one; [17]and take the helmet of salvation, and the sword of the Spirit, which is the word of God, [18]praying at all times in the Spirit, with all prayer and supplication.

2 Corinthians 12:1-10

I must go on boasting. Though there is nothing to be gained by it, I will go on to visions and revelations of the Lord. [2]I know a man in Christ who fourteen years ago was caught up to the third heaven—whether in the body or out of the body I do not know, God knows. [3]And I know that this man was caught up into paradise—whether in the body or out of the body I do not know, God knows— [4]and he heard things that cannot be told, which man may not utter. [5]On behalf of this man I will boast, but on my own behalf I will not boast, except of my weaknesses. [6]Though if I should wish to boast, I would not be a fool, for I would be speaking the truth. But I refrain from it, so that no one may think more of me than he sees in me or hears from me. [7]So to keep me from being too elated by the surpassing greatness of the revelations, a thorn was given me in the flesh, a messenger of Satan to harass me, to keep me from being too elated. [8]Three times I pleaded with the Lord about this, that it should leave me. [9]But he said to me, "My grace is sufficient for you, for my power is made perfect in weakness." Therefore I will boast all the more gladly of my weaknesses, so that the power of Christ may rest upon me. [10]For the sake of Christ, then, I am content with weaknesses, insults, hardships, persecutions, and calamities. For when I am weak, then I am strong.

2 Corinthians 10:3-5

For though we walk in the flesh, we are not waging war according to the flesh. [4]For the weapons of our warfare are not of the flesh but have divine power to destroy strongholds. [5]We destroy arguments and every lofty opinion raised against the knowledge of God, and take every thought captive to obey Christ.

Romans 13:12

The night is far gone; the day is at hand. So then let us cast off the works of darkness and put on the armor of light.

1 Thessalonians 5:8

But since we belong to the day, let us be sober, having put on the breastplate of faith and love, and for a helmet the hope of salvation.

1 Timothy 6:12

Fight the good fight of the faith. Take hold of the eternal life to which you were called and about which you made the good confession in the presence of many witnesses.

2 Timothy 2:3-4

Share in suffering as a good soldier of Christ Jesus. [4]No soldier gets entangled in civilian pursuits, since his aim is to please the one who enlisted him.

1 Peter 5:8-11

Be sober-minded; be watchful. Your adversary the devil prowls around like a roaring lion, seeking someone to devour. [9]Resist him, firm in your faith, knowing that the same kinds of suffering are being experienced by your brotherhood throughout the world. [10]And after you have suffered a little while, the God of all grace, who has called you to his eternal glory in Christ, will himself restore, confirm, strengthen, and establish you. [11]To him be the dominion forever and ever. Amen.

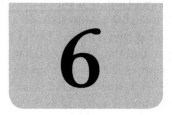

CHAPTER

6

~~~~~~~~~~~~~~~~~~~~~~~~
Progress Memory Verse

*For though we walk in the flesh, we are not waging war according
to the flesh. For the weapons of our warfare are not of the flesh but
have divine power to destroy strongholds.*

– 2 Corinthians 10:3-4

~~~~~~~~~~~~~~~~~~~~~~~~

TO BEGIN

Have you passed through truly dark times in life? How has God encouraged you?

THE VALLEY OF HUMILIATION AND APOLLYON

1. After seasons of favor, God's pilgrims can succumb to a great plague of the heart -- pride. For our own good, therefore, God lets us descend into humbling circumstances. For most of us, learning humility is a difficult process. How does 1 Peter 5:5-7 encourage you?

2. (*) In Deuteronomy 8, God explains why He led the children of Israel through the wilderness. What did He intend to teach them and for what reasons? (See vss.2-3, 16-20.)

3. In the Valley of Humiliation, the evil enemy Apollyon confronts Christian. What is Apollyon's goal? (See 1 Peter 5:8.)

4. Apollyon's strategy to recapture Christian begins with gentle persuasion and then escalates to a war of words. What tactics does he use in his attempt to reclaim Christian? Underline those to which you might feel vulnerable, and pray over these.

5. How does Christian reply to Apollyon's accusations against Christ? How does Christian reply to Apollyon's accusations against himself (Christian)?

Against Christ:

Against himself (Christian):

~~~~~~~~~~~~~~~~~~~~~~~~

Definition: Apollyon

The name Apollyon means "destroyer." The Apostle John, in Revelation 9:11, calls him an angel who is the king of the bottomless pit. He also explains that the name in Hebrew is Abaddon and in Greek is Apollyon. This fallen angel leads a legion of demonic entities that swarm like "locusts" to wreak havoc on the earth.

~~~~~~~~~~~~~~~~~~~~~~~~

THE INEVITABLE CONFLICT

6. When all else fails, Apollyon flies into a rage and spreads himself across the King's Highway. What is this tactic, and how can this be effective against us in our battles?

7. Christian wasn't looking for trouble when he unexpectedly found himself in mortal combat. According to Judges 3:1-2 and Ephesians 6:11-13, why might God allow this turn of events in a Christian's life?

8. Why couldn't Christian simply run from this threat? Consider the armor listed in Ephesians 6:14-18. What vital area is not covered? Have you ever attempted to turn to find an easier way only to find yourself shot full of arrows?

~~~~~~~~~~~~~~~~~~~~~~~~

Progress Quote from Another Pilgrim

Spiritual warfare is very real. There is a furious, fierce, and ferocious battle raging in the realm of the spirit between the forces of God and the forces of evil. Warfare happens every day, all the time. Whether you believe it or not, you are in a battlefield. You are in warfare."

--Pedro Okoro

~~~~~~~~~~~~~~~~~~~~~~~~

9. Apollyon wounds Christian in three places – his head, his hand, and his foot. If wounding to the head represents a blow to Christian's ability to understand and think clearly, what might wounds to the hand and foot mean?

    Hand:

    Foot:

10. (*) What do you think Bunyan is trying to convey when he says the conflict went on for more than half a day until Christian lost his sword?

11. Right when things seemed worst for Christian in his spiritual battle, we see the wonderful words, "But, as God would have it", Christian grabbed his sword and defeated his enemy. How does this encourage you for your own battles? Can you think of a time when you felt like you were going down in defeat but the Holy Spirit brought you a special promise to encourage you? Record it here:

12. God does not give believers weapons for play but for battle. It is a modern misconception that life should be easy. A battle rages for the souls of humanity. Have you taken your enemy too lightly? Have you been on a battlefield without your armor? How can you better equip yourself for victory?

13. (*) Ephesians 6:17 calls God's Word "the sword of the Spirit." In Luke 4:1-13, how many times did our Lord Jesus wield the sword of Scripture against the devil? How do you think studying, memorizing, believing, and speaking God's Word can help you in your spiritual battles?

~~~~~~~~~~~~~~~~~~~~~~~~~~~~~~~

Progress Tip

Don't be surprised when you feel you are in a tug-of-war between God's Spirit leading you forward and the devil trying to stop or hinder you. Choose progress! Be prepared with your armor on and weapon drawn; be prepared to fight your way through. This way, the devil's efforts may slow you down, but he can never stop you. You will emerge from your trial victorious.

~~~~~~~~~~~~~~~~~~~~~~~~~~~~~~~

14. James 4:7 promises that if we submit to God and resist the devil, the devil must flee. Decide right now to use this promise (and others) as a "sword of the Spirit" against your enemy. Write a faith declaration and claim it against your area of vulnerability. (Sample: "I submit my entire life to the Lord. According to His promise, I command you, spirit of darkness, to release me and to leave me right now in the mighty Name of Jesus! Thank you, Jesus, for my victory! Amen!")

HEALING

15. Note that Christian had a part to play. How did he receive healing and comfort? What do you think were some areas that God healed? How do you see this applying to your own life?

16. Did Christian's healing mean he thought that his battles were all behind him? What did he do about that? What can you do similarly?

THE VALLEY OF THE SHADOW OF DEATH

17. Things seem to go from bad to worse in the Valley of the Shadow of Death. How is this valley described? To what type of difficult time in the Christian life might this allude? Why would you think it is called a "Shadow"?

18. Why do you think Bunyan says that only a Christian passes this way, and what lesson is he seeking to communicate?

19. (*) Two apostates --"Descendants of the Spies" -- confront Christian with a terrifying account of what's ahead. When Moses sent twelve men to spy out the Promised Land, ten came back with an evil report. How did this influence the community? (See Numbers 13:25-33;14:1-4.) How could such "descendants" sway Christians today? How does Christian respond to the report given him?

20. What do you think the ditch and the quagmire represent? What is the safest place for pilgrims as they move forward? Why is this place so narrow?

    Ditch:

    Quagmire:

    Safe place:

21. Surrounded by a "band of Fiends," Christian heard blasphemous voices and mistook them for his own voice. He even thought he had committed blasphemy! Can believers today be vulnerable to such episodes? How can we fortify ourselves against such attacks?

22. What does the Mouth of Hell represent? When all else seemed to fail, what helps Christian come through this place?

23. What kinds of inner conflicts can the Valley of the Shadow of Death represent for Christians?

24. When Christian heard someone ahead quoting Psalm 23:4, he felt encouraged. What reasons are given for his feeling?

~~~~~~

Key Pilgrim's Perspective

God has charted a roadmap for each of us. We might want our way to be happy and carefree; but we are in training, and the narrow way is never easy. Our training is often humbling, but Scripture assures us that "humility comes before honor" (Proverbs 15:33; 18:12). In these difficult places, dark forces may assail us, and darkness may engulf us; but we should not give up. God is with us and will lead us safely through. True, we may experience pain and trauma; in the end, however, we will find ourselves more God-reliant, courageous, faith filled, and rich in hope. As we look back, we see real progress. We are learning that God's grace in us conquers the challenges of Apollyon and the Valley of the Shadow of Death. We realize that God has been there all along, weaving everything into His plan for our ultimate good. Remember that the strongest pilgrims, like refined metal, are those who have passed through fires of adversity.

~~~~~~

25. Christian came through his experience more humble, wise, pure, and prayerful. Can you think of times you came through a Valley of the Shadow of Death experience and saw things differently in the light of day? Can you look back and see that God used your adversity for good in your life? Describe:

~~~~~~~~~~~~~~~~~~~~~~~~~~~~~

Scriptures for Further Reflection

1 John 4:4, 5:4
John 8:44
Luke 4:4-8
Ephesians 2:1-6
1 Peter 5:8-11
Isaiah 41:11-13
Psalm 32:7; 138:6-8

~~~~~~~~~~~~~~~~~~~~~~~~~~~~~

NOTES:

_____

_____

_____

_____

_____

_____

_____

_____

_____

_____

_____

_____

_____

_____

_____

_____

_____

_____

SCRIPTURES USED IN THIS CHAPTER

1 Peter 5:5-7

Likewise, you who are younger, be subject to the elders. Clothe yourselves, all of you, with humility toward one another, for "God opposes the proud but gives grace to the humble." [6]Humble yourselves, therefore, under the mighty hand of God so that at the proper time he may exalt you, [7]casting all your anxieties on him, because he cares for you.

Deuteronomy 8:2-3, 16-20

And you shall remember the whole way that the LORD your God has led you these forty years in the wilderness, that he might humble you, testing you to know what was in your heart, whether you would keep his commandments or not. [3]And he humbled you and let you hunger and fed you with manna, which you did not know, nor did your fathers know, that he might make you know that man does not live by bread alone, but man lives by every word that comes from the mouth of the LORD . . . . [16](He) fed you in the wilderness with manna that your fathers did not know, that he might humble you and test you, to do you good in the end. [17]Beware lest you say in your heart, 'My power and the might of my hand have gotten me this wealth.' [18]You shall remember the LORD your God, for it is he who gives you power to get wealth, that he may confirm his covenant that he swore to your fathers, as it is this day. [19]And if you forget the LORD your God and go after other gods and serve them and worship them, I solemnly warn you today that you shall surely perish. [20]Like the nations that the LORD makes to perish before you, so shall you perish, because you would not obey the voice of the LORD your God.

1 Peter 5:8

Be sober-minded; be watchful. Your adversary the devil prowls around like a roaring lion, seeking someone to devour.

Judges 3:1-2

Now these are the nations that the LORD left, to test Israel by them, that is, all in Israel who had not experienced all the wars in Canaan. [2]It was only in order that the generations of the people of Israel might know war, to teach war to those who had not known it before.

Ephesians 6:11-13

Put on the whole armor of God, that you may be able to stand against the schemes of the devil. [12]For we do not wrestle against flesh and blood, but against the rulers, against the authorities, against the cosmic powers over this present darkness, against the spiritual forces of evil in the heavenly places. [13]Therefore take up the whole armor of God, that you may be able to withstand in the evil day, and having done all, to stand firm.

Ephesians 6:14-18

Stand therefore, having fastened on the belt of truth, and having put on the breastplate of righteousness, [15]and, as shoes for your feet, having put on the readiness given by the gospel of peace. [16]In all circumstances take up the shield of faith, with which you can extinguish all the flaming darts of the evil one; [17]and take the helmet of salvation, and the sword of the Spirit, which is the word of God, [18]praying at all times in the Spirit, with all prayer and supplication. To that end keep alert with all perseverance, making supplication for all the saints.

Luke 4:1-13

And Jesus, full of the Holy Spirit, returned from the Jordan and was led by the Spirit in the wilderness [2]for forty days, being tempted by the devil. And he ate nothing during those days. And when they were ended, he was hungry. [3]The devil said to him, "If you are the Son of God, command this stone to become bread." [4]And Jesus answered him, "It is written, 'Man shall not live by bread alone.'" [5]And the devil took him up and showed him all the kingdoms of the world in a moment of time, [6]and said to him, "To you I will give all this authority and their glory, for it has been delivered to me, and I give it to whom I will. [7]If you, then, will worship me, it will all be yours." [8]And Jesus answered him, "It is written, "'You shall worship the Lord your God, and him only shall you serve.'" [9]And he took him to Jerusalem and set him on the pinnacle of the temple and said to him, "If you are the Son of God, throw yourself down from here, [10]for it is written, "'He will command his angels concerning you, to guard you,' [11]and "'On their hands they will bear you up, lest you strike your foot against a stone.'" [12]And Jesus answered him, "It is said, 'You shall not put the Lord your God to the test.'" [13]And when the devil had ended every temptation, he departed from him until an opportune time.

James 4:7

Submit yourselves therefore to God. Resist the devil, and he will flee from you.

Numbers 13:25-33; 14:1-4

At the end of forty days they returned from spying out the land. [26]And they came to Moses and Aaron and to all the congregation of the people of Israel in the wilderness of Paran, at Kadesh. They brought back word to them and to all the congregation, and showed them the fruit of the land. [27]And they told him, "We came to the land to which you sent us. It flows with milk and honey, and this is its fruit. [28]However, the people who dwell in the land are strong, and the cities are fortified and very large. And besides, we saw the descendants of Anak there. [29]The Amalekites dwell in the land of the Negeb. The Hittites, the Jebusites, and the Amorites dwell in the hill country. And the Canaanites dwell by the sea, and along the Jordan." [30]But Caleb quieted the people before Moses and said, "Let us go up at once and occupy it, for we are well able to overcome it." [31]Then the men who had gone up with him said, "We are not able to go up against the people, for they are stronger than we are." [32]So they brought to the people of Israel a bad report of the land that they had spied out, saying, "The land, through which we have gone to spy it out, is a land that devours its inhabitants, and all the people that we saw in it are of great height. [33]And there we saw the Nephilim (the sons of Anak, who come from the Nephilim), and we seemed to ourselves like grasshoppers, and so we seemed to them." [14:1]Then all the congregation raised a loud cry, and the people wept that night. [2]And all the people of Israel grumbled against Moses and Aaron. The whole congregation said to them, "Would that we had died in the land of Egypt! Or would that we had died in this wilderness! [3]Why is the LORD bringing us into this land, to fall by the sword? Our wives and our little ones will become a prey. Would it not be better for us to go back to Egypt?" [4]And they said to one another, "Let us choose a leader and go back to Egypt."

Psalm 23:4

Even though I walk through the valley of the shadow of death, I will fear no evil, for you are with me; your rod and your staff, they comfort me.

2 Corinthians 10:3-4 (Memory verse)

For though we walk in the flesh, we are not waging war according to the flesh. [4]For the weapons of our warfare are not of the flesh but have divine power to destroy strongholds.

CHAPTER

~~~~~~~~~~~~~~~~~~~~~~~~~~~~

Progress Memory Verse

No temptation has taken you except what is common to man. God is faithful, who will not allow you to be tempted above what you are able, but will with the temptation also make the way of escape, that you may be able to endure it.

--1 Corinthians 10:13

~~~~~~~~~~~~~~~~~~~~~~~~~~~~

TO BEGIN

Can you describe a time when you went through something humbling, not because of any mistake on your part but because it was God's will?

CHRISTIAN AND FAITHFUL MEET IN THE WAY

1. In Chapter 6, Apollyon had accused Christian of a secret vulnerability to self-glory, and Christian proves his point. How is he humbled, and how might Proverbs 16:18 have helped him?

2. What resulted from Christian stumbling after he ran past Faithful, and what can we learn from it?

NEWS FROM HOME

3. Christian caused a stir by leaving the City of Destruction. According to Faithful, how did most people respond?

4. If Christian thought his witness in the City of Destruction was fruitless, he was wrong. Why? How does this encourage you?

Progress Quote from Another Pilgrim

Only he who flings himself upward when the pull comes to drag him down, can hope to break the force of temptation. Temptation may be an invitation to Hell, but much more is it an opportunity to reach heaven.

--Charles H. Brent

FAITHFUL'S CONFRONTATIONS WITH TEMPTATION

5. **First temptation:**

   a. What is it?

   b. How is it described, and what does it offer?

   c. How does Faithful escape this temptation?

   d. In what ways do you see the temptation brought by Wanton prevalent in the world today? How would you advise people to resist it? What advice does Psalm 119:9 give?

6. **Second temptation:**

   a. What is it?

   b. How is it described, and what does it offer?

c. How does Faithful escape this temptation?

~~~~~~~~~~~~~~~~~~~~~~~~~~

Definition: Old Man

This label is found In Romans 6:6, Ephesians 4:22, and Colossians 3:9, particularly in the King James Version. It refers not to physical age but to the spiritual condition of a corrupt fallen nature. Other translations render it variously, "the old self," "the old nature," and "the old sinful nature." This is the nature that has governed unredeemed humanity since the fall in the Garden when "Adam the First" yielded to the devil and brought sin and destruction. It opposes "the new man" within us that Christ, "the last Adam," (1 Corinthians 15:45) purchased for us.

~~~~~~~~~~~~~~~~~~~~~~~~~~

d. In what ways do you see the temptation brought by the Old Man prevalent in the world today? How would you advise people to resist it?

7. **Third temptation:**

a. What is it?

b. How is it described, and what does it offer?

c. How does Faithful escape this temptation?

d. In what ways do you see the temptation brought by Moses prevalent in the world today? How would you advise people to resist it?

e. Let's look back again at the Law of Moses for a moment. Paul describes a great conflict in Romans 7 that centers in the Law. What does v. 12 say about it? Truly, God's Law is so holy that it can leave us, like Faithful, knocked flat on our back in despair. In view of this, how does the Lord's grace make Paul feel? How should it make you feel? (See Romans 7:24-25 & 8:1.)

8. **Fourth temptation:**

   a. What is it?

   b. How is it described, and what does it offer?

   c. How does Faithful escape this temptation?

   d. In what ways do you see the temptation brought by Discontent prevalent in the world today? How would you advise people to resist it?

9. **Fifth temptation:**

   a. What is it?

   b. How is it described, and what does it offer?

Progress Tip

To be tempted is no sin. Opening our heart to temptation and yielding to it-- that is sin and should be feared. When you are confronted with temptation, pray for grace to withstand it, and don't grow discouraged in your resisting. Every moment you fend off the temptation is a triumph that will bring you increasing strength, victory, and progress.

~~~~~~~~~~~~~~~~~~~~~~~

c.   How does Faithful escape this temptation?

d.   In what ways do you see this temptation brought by Shame prevalent in the world today? How would you advise people to resist it? How did Jesus warn against Shame in Mark 8:38, and how does Paul respond in Romans 1:16?

~~~~~~

Key Pilgrim's Perspective

The Valley of Humiliation devastates our pride. Here, we recognize and admit truth vital to our pilgrimage: First, the world's arguments, pleas, and pretenses are extremely convincing. Second, our heart's depravity, deceitfulness, and rebellion are exceedingly pervasive. And, third, our soul's spiritual enemies are intensely subtle, convincing, and powerful. In short, the world, the flesh, and the devil conspire against us, using potent temptations suited to our own vulnerabilities. We must not treat them lightly!

Never be casual about temptation. Sin is never a small thing. The devil whispers through the keyhole of our hearts, "Let me in, for I have goods to sell you that will make life easier and happier for you." But if we crack the door open for this shrewd salesman, he will take it as an open invitation and get his foot in the door. He will then force his way in, sell us his snake oil, and ruin us. Instead, we must command the enemy to leave, and we must rely upon the grace of Jesus Christ to keep us safe.

No one alive is immune to the power of temptation. We can all be broken down and fall under its spell. As bad as things may seem, however, God's Word assures us that our temptation is neither unusual nor insurmountable. He has provided breakthroughs for us. The question is will we choose them?

~~~~~~

A PERSONAL LOOK AT TEMPTATION

10. We note that Christian and Faithful's trials and temptations varied. How does this relate to us?

11. How are you doing with the temptations that came at Faithful? (See list below.) Have you conquered them, or do you find they don't much bother you? How can you better walk in victory over them?

    a. Wanton

    b. The Old Man

    c. Moses

    d. Discontent

    e. Shame

12. (*) As you have progressed on your pilgrimage, are there other temptations that have pummeled you? How are you mastering them?

13. Do temptations sometimes discourage you? How do Hebrews 2:18 and 4:15 encourage you?

14. How can you make an effort to become more aware of temptations this week and to resist them?

~~~~~~~~~~~~~~~~~~~~~~~~~

Scriptures for Further Reflection

Luke 14:7-11
Psalm 133:1
Acts 18:6
Proverbs 5:1-23
1 John 2:15-17
Romans 5:14-21
Hebrews 12:2
Luke 22:45-46
James 1:12-16

~~~~~~~~~~~~~~~~~~~~~~~~~

NOTES:

SCRIPTURES USED IN THIS CHAPTER

Proverbs 16:18
Pride goes before destruction, and a haughty spirit before a fall.

Psalm 119:9-11
How can a young man keep his way pure? By guarding it according to your word. [10] With my whole heart I seek you; let me not wander from your commandments![11] I have stored up your word in my heart, that I might not sin against you.

Romans 7:12, 24-25
So the law is holy, and the commandment is holy and righteous and good. . . . [24]Wretched man that I am! Who will deliver me from this body of death? [25]Thanks be to God through Jesus Christ our Lord! So then, I myself serve the law of God with my mind, but with my flesh I serve the law of sin.

Romans 8:1
There is therefore now no condemnation for those who are in Christ Jesus.

Mark 8:38
For whoever is ashamed of me and of my words in this adulterous and sinful generation, of him will the Son of Man also be ashamed when he comes in the glory of his Father with the holy angels.

Romans 1: 16 NLT
For I am not ashamed of this Good News about Christ. It is the power of God at work, saving everyone who believes — the Jew first and also the Gentile.

Hebrews 2:18
For because he himself has suffered when tempted, he is able to help those who are being tempted.

Hebrews 4:15
For we do not have a high priest who is unable to sympathize with our weaknesses, but one who in every respect has been tempted as we are, yet without sin.

CHAPTER

8

TO BEGIN

There's an old '60s song, "You Talk Too Much." It begins, "You talk too much, you worry me to death; You talk too much, you even worry my pet . . ." How do you feel about people who talk too much? Do you sometimes enjoy talking too much?

FAITHFUL AND TALKATIVE

1. What does Talkative's name indicate about him right away?

2. As Faithful and Talkative begin their first discussion, Faithful clarifies the purpose he sees in this. What is it?

CHRISTIAN AND FAITHFUL DISCUSS TALKATIVE

3. Christian seemed rather judgmental toward Talkative. Today, many would accuse him of intolerance and contend that God's people should never judge others. How does Ephesians 5:6-17 moderate this view?

4. When Christian judges Talkative as a hypocrite, why doesn't he think this qualifies as slander?

5. What were some of Christian's reasons for viewing Talkative as a hypocrite?

~~~~~~~~~~~~~~~~~~~~~~~

Definition: Hypocrite

A hypocrite is one who professes beliefs, feelings, or virtues without truly possessing them or living them out. This person wears a mask and feigns to be what he is not. His actions belie his stated beliefs. The label actually derives from the Greek word hupokrinomai – to speak on stage, to impersonate, and play a part. Ancient Greeks called their actors hypocrites.

Jesus often called religious leaders hypocrites, e.g., in Matthew 15:7, 22:18, 23:13; Luke 12:56. He also warned His followers against hypocrisy, e.g., Matthew 6:2, 5,16.

~~~~~~~~~~~~~~~~~~~~~~~

6. Christian contends that on Judgment Day we will all be judged by our fruit. How does Christ address this issue in Matthew 7:15-20?

7. How does Christian relate words and deeds to soul and body? What does he say the soul of true faith is?

8. According to Paul, what is the relationship between salvation by grace and good works? (See Ephesians 2:8-10.)

9. (*) Christian cites a portion of 1 Corinthians 13:1, calling those like Talkative "resounding gongs and clanging cymbals." How does this description fit the man?

10. 1 Corinthians 13:1 also tells us that love is the crucial quality that the "resounding gongs and clanging cymbals" lack. 1 Corinthians 13:4-7 describes the manifestations of love. Which of these love-traits is hardest for you? Can you think of specific ways to work on these in the coming weeks?

FAITHFUL CONFRONTS TALKATIVE'S ERROR

11. Faithful and Talkative discuss how they each believe saving grace is revealed in one's heart. Talkative gives two ways, and Faithful refutes them both. What are they?

    a.

    b.

12. According to Faithful, what is the difference between crying out against sin and abhorring it?

13. Why does Bunyan distinguish between two kinds of knowledge?

14. Think about your biblical knowledge. Are you allowing it to make a permanent impact on the way you live? List some practical ways in which you can better conform your life to God's Word.

15. Faithful describes how a true work of grace in the heart manifests itself. He contends there are two ways it shows itself in a life. What are they?

    a.

    b.

16. How have you seen the work of grace manifested in your own life? Be sure to thank God right now for this grace and to ask for even richer manifestations.

TALKATIVE CHOOSES TO PART COMPANY

17. (*) Christian and Faithful were happy to separate from Talkative. We should stay away from certain people for our own good. Why? (See 1 Corinthians 15:33.)

18. Despite the sour ending to the conversation between Faithful and Talkative, why is Faithful satisfied?

19. Christian praises Faithful for confronting Talkative. He wishes all hypocrites received this kind of treatment. Why?

20. If we keep company with hypocrites, how will the world evaluate us? How does Romans 2:17-24 speak to this?

~~~~~~

Key Pilgrim's Perspective

The craving for popularity has wrecked the lives of more professing Christians than outward persecution ever has. Indeed, people like Talkative starve without an audience. Feeding on admiration, they find far more satisfaction in hearing themselves talk than in hearing God talk. Enthralled with their conversation and not their conversion, such people cannot bear fruit that doesn't contain worms and rottenness. True pilgrims want to influence people to come to Christ and not to themselves.

We don't assess fruitfulness in the Christian life by what we say we believe. We measure it, rather, by how we love, exalt Christ, and build His Kingdom. If we serve the Lord with only our lips, we are self-deceived in a way that leaves us full of ourselves, yet empty and fruitless. But if we allow God's presence and love to fill our service to Him and others, we will have a blessed and fruitful pilgrimage.

~~~~~~

21. Besides saying the right words, how does 1 Timothy 4:12 instruct us to communicate our faith?

22. While we are to evaluate others, we also can expect them to evaluate us. Based on Matthew 5:16, what efforts will you make to shine your light in a way that honors and glorifies God?

~~~~~~~~~~~~~~~~~~~~~~~~~~~~~

Scriptures for Further Reflection

1 Corinthians 2:4; 4:20
Psalm 26:4
Matthew 6:5
Mark 7:6
2 Timothy 1:5
James 2:18-26

~~~~~~~~~~~~~~~~~~~~~~~~~~~~~

NOTES:

_____

_____

_____

_____

_____

_____

_____

_____

_____

_____

_____

_____

_____

_____

_____

_____

_____

_____

_____

_____

_____

SCRIPTURES USED IN THIS CHAPTER

Ephesians 5:6-17 WEB

Let no one deceive you with empty words. For because of these things, the wrath of God comes on the children of disobedience. [7]Therefore don't be partakers with them. [8]For you were once darkness, but are now light in the Lord. Walk as children of light, [9]for the fruit of the Spirit is in all goodness and righteousness and truth, [10]proving what is well pleasing to the Lord. [11]Have no fellowship with the unfruitful deeds of darkness, but rather even reprove them. [12]For it is a shame even to speak of the things which are done by them in secret. [13]But all things, when they are reproved, are revealed by the light, for everything that reveals is light. [14]Therefore he says, "Awake, you who sleep, and arise from the dead, and Christ will shine on you."[15]Therefore watch carefully how you walk, not as unwise, but as wise, [16]redeeming the time, because the days are evil. [17]Therefore don't be foolish, but understand what the will of the Lord is.

Matthew 7:15-20

"Beware of false prophets, who come to you in sheep's clothing but inwardly are ravenous wolves. [16]You will recognize them by their fruits. Are grapes gathered from thornbushes, or figs from thistles? [17]So, every healthy tree bears good fruit, but the diseased tree bears bad fruit. [18] A healthy tree cannot bear bad fruit, nor can a diseased tree bear good fruit. [19]Every tree that does not bear good fruit is cut down and thrown into the fire. [20]Thus you will recognize them by their fruits.

Ephesians 2:8-10

For by grace you have been saved through faith. And this is not your own doing; it is the gift of God, [9]not a result of works, so that no one may boast. [10]For we are his workmanship, created in Christ Jesus for good works, which God prepared beforehand, that we should walk in them.

1 Corinthians 13:1 NIV

If I speak in the tongues of men and of angels, but have not love, I am only a resounding gong or a clanging cymbal.

1 Corinthians 13: 4-7 NIV

Love is patient, love is kind. It does not envy, it does not boast, it is not proud. [5]It is not rude, it is not self-seeking, it is not easily angered, it keeps no record of wrongs. [6]Love does not delight in evil but rejoices with the truth. [7]It always protects, always trusts, always hopes, always perseveres.

1 Corinthians 15:33 NIV

Do not be misled: "Bad company corrupts good character."

Romans 2:17-24

But if you call yourself a Jew and rely on the law and boast in God [18]and know his will and approve what is excellent, because you are instructed from the law; [19]and if you are sure that you yourself are a guide to the blind, a light to those who are in darkness, [20]an instructor of the foolish, a teacher of children, having in the law the embodiment of knowledge and truth—[21]you then who teach others, do you not teach yourself? While you preach against stealing, do you steal? [22]You who say that one must not commit adultery, do you commit adultery? You who abhor idols, do you rob temples? [23]You who boast in the law dishonor God by breaking the law. [24]For, as it is written, "The name of God is blasphemed among the Gentiles because of you."

1 Timothy 4:12

Let no one despise you for your youth, but set the believers an example in speech, in conduct, in love, in faith, in purity.

Matthew 5:16

In the same way, let your light shine before others, so that they may see your good works and give glory to your Father who is in heaven.

Colossians 4:2-6

Continue steadfastly in prayer, being watchful in it with thanksgiving. [3]At the same time, pray also for us, that God may open to us a door for the word, to declare the mystery of Christ, on account of which I am in prison— [4]that I may make it clear, which is how I ought to speak. [5]Conduct yourselves wisely toward outsiders, making the best use of the time. [6]Let your speech always be gracious, seasoned with salt, so that you may know how you ought to answer each person.

James 2:17, 26

So also faith by itself, if it does not have works, is dead. . . [26]For as the body apart from the spirit is dead, so also faith apart from works is dead.

CHAPTER

~~~~~~~~~~~~~~~~~~~~~~~~~~~
Progress Quote from Another Pilgrim

When Christ calls a man, He bids him come and die.

— Dietrich Bonhoeffer, *The Cost of Discipleship*

~~~~~~~~~~~~~~~~~~~~~~~~~~~

TO BEGIN

Have you been in a place like Vanity Fair? Describe the situation.

EVANGELIST ENCOURAGES THE PILGRIMS

1. What was there about Christian and Faithful's progress thus far that made Evangelist "very happy?"

2. As any good mentor would do, Evangelist admonishes the pilgrims in a number of ways. What are some things he said? Also, how did he encourage them?

~~~~~~~~~~~~~~~~~~~~~~~~~

Progress Memory Verses

I am coming quickly! Hold firmly that which you have, so that no one takes your crown. --Revelation 3:11

Yes, and all who desire to live godly in Christ Jesus will suffer persecution. –2 Timothy 3:12

~~~~~~~~~~~~~~~~~~~~~~~~~

3. We should seek to be peacemakers in this world, but it is no easy task. According to 1 Peter 2:11, what is your relationship to the world? Since this is true, is Christ's ultimate goal for you to live harmoniously with the world? Based on John 15:18-20, what can you expect from the world?

4. Evangelist includes Revelation 3:11 in his admonition to the pilgrims. What hope and what warning does this Scripture express? What does this mean for Christians today?

5. Consider further the issue of crowns by reading 1 Corinthians 9:24-27. How can this relate to your own pilgrimage? What will you seek to do this week in response?

6. Flint is a hard stone. It remains unyielding when most anything comes up against it. Evangelist warned the pilgrims to set their faces like flint toward their destination. In other words, no matter what, they must keep their eyes fixed on their goal and not get diverted. How did Isaiah use flint to illustrate resolve in Isaiah 50:7? Read about the Apostle Paul in Philippians. 3:13-16. How did he resolve to keep progressing in his life and ministry, and how does he urge us concerning our own progress?

7. Evangelist is also a prophet. What did he prophesy? What further exhortation does he give?

8. Paul declared, "For me to live is Christ, and to die is gain" (Philippians. 1:21). He said he was willing to die for Christ, and he meant it. Ultimately, God carries us through severe trials. Nevertheless, can you think of ways to fortify your heart in the event of painful persecution?

9. How does Evangelist's exhortation related to persecution counter the beliefs of some Christians about lives that are blessed?

~~~~~~~~~~~~~~~~~~~~~~~~~

Definition - Vanity

Today, more often than not, we think of vanity as it relates to prideful and conceited people. The biblical meaning, however, is different. For instance, when Ecclesiastes 1:2 says, "Vanity of vanities! All is vanity," it uses the Hebrew word *hebel*, meaning vapor or breath. It derives from another word, *habal*, which indicates emptiness, futility, worthlessness, and being led astray.

~~~~~~~~~~~~~~~~~~~~~~~~~

VANITY FAIR

10. The storyteller says we must all pass through Vanity Fair and that even our Lord Jesus, "the Prince of Princes," could not escape it. He, of course, refused the Fair's vanities. Drawing from our Lord's example in Matthew 4:1-11, how did He avoid entanglement in "Vanity Fair," and how can we?

11. The pilgrims entered Vanity Fair and caused an immediate stir. What three reasons are given for this, and what do they represent?

    a.

    b.

    c

12. (*) Ephesians 2:1-9 present the differences between those who walk "according to the course of this world" and those who choose Christ's way. What are some of those differences?

13. The pilgrims caused a commotion because they were different. Do Christians in present-day society cause a commotion, or are we largely ignored? Do you see attitudes changing? What kind of opposition do Christians face here and abroad?

~~~~~~

A Helpful Exhortation

Love not the world. Don't love the world's ways. Don't love the world's goods. Love of the world squeezes out love for the Father. Practically everything that goes on in the world—wanting your own way, wanting everything for yourself, wanting to appear important—has nothing to do with the Father. It just isolates you from Him. The world and all its wanting, wanting, wanting is on the way out—but whoever does what God wants is set for eternity.

--1 John 2:15-17 MSG

~~~~~~

14. What variety of seductive worldly allurements get displayed at the fair! Jesus speaks to this danger in Mark 4:18-19. Today's culture seems to present a proliferation of temptations to "choke the Word." Can you think of particular things that choke life out of God's people?

15. Considering the danger, we should be careful that things don't own us but rather that we own them. What are some things that most entice your heart, and what do you intend to do about it?

16. Perhaps the material things of Vanity Fair do not entice you so much as do other fine wares that swell the ego. How do earthly positions, honors, promotions, or titles influence you? You may be called to push these things aside for the sake of a faithful pilgrimage. Are you willing to do that?

17. Can you think of any other worldly enticements and fears that might hinder your spiritual progress? How can you die to these things and live more boldly for Christ? Rely on the Holy Spirit's inspiration right now, and make some goals for your progress over the coming weeks.

18. Shunning the fair and its vanities, the pilgrims declared, "We will buy the truth!" (See Proverbs 23:23.) Today, in a land awash in sin and falsehood, and with increasing opposition toward righteousness, Christians can still "buy truth" and secure it. Name some ways in which this is done:

~~~~~~~~~~~~~~~~~~~~~~~~~~~

Progress Tip

Do you sometimes feel your suffering makes no sense – that it is due either to a cosmic mistake or some unfathomable punishment from God?

Romans 5:3-5 says we should rejoice at our sufferings since they produce endurance; and endurance produces character; and character, hope. It concludes that hope will never disappoint us. Why? Our sufferings convince us that what we hope for will be fulfilled, and the Holy Spirit gives us an overwhelming experience of God's love.

Your suffering, therefore, works towards a victorious and joyful end to your pilgrimage. Keep this in mind when trials assail you.

~~~~~~~~~~~~~~~~~~~~~~~~~~~

19. (*) When God's people stand for biblical truth and morality, they can expect retaliation. An old adage asks, "If you were arrested for being a Christian, would there be enough evidence to convict you?" How would you answer this question?

~~~~~~

Key Pilgrim's Perspective

When a disciple named Ananias heard God call him to go and bless a certain new convert, he expressed dismay.

God replied, *"Go! This man is my chosen instrument to carry my name before the Gentiles and their kings and before the people of Israel. I will show him how much he must suffer for my name"* (Acts 9:15-16). This man, of course, would become the great Apostle Paul.

Much later, a prophet named Agabus foretold of great opposition against Paul should he go to Jerusalem. Friends interpreted this to mean he should stay away from there. Convinced, however, that his path led through Jerusalem, Paul refused their warning. As it turned out, great opposition *did* greet him in Jerusalem. But this path also provided the open door through which he would fulfill his destiny to present the Gospel to Roman kings. (See Acts 21-26.)

By the time Paul wrote the book of 2 Timothy, he had served God's Kingdom intensely for more than thirty years. From personal experience, he could unequivocally declare, *Yes, and all who desire to live godly in Christ Jesus will suffer persecution* (2 Timothy 3:12). While Paul, indeed, suffered great persecution, just look at his fruit! God's faithful pilgrims should look to Paul's example, not to those so-called pilgrims who have comfortably settled in Vanity Fair.

~~~~~~

CHRISTIAN AND FAITHFUL STAND TRIAL

20. The poor pilgrims, especially Faithful! Vanity's court with its judge (Lord Hate-good), witnesses (Envy, Superstition, and Talebearer), and jurors (Messrs. Blind-man, No-good, Malice, Love-lust, Live-loose, Heady, High-mind, Enmity, Liar, Cruelty, Hate-light, and Implacable) assure injustice. These names represent the true reasons that God's people are on trial in this world. Which, if any, have ever "indicted" you? How willing are you to receive a "guilty" verdict and be convicted of crimes worthy of true pilgrims?

21. How did it really end for Faithful?

~~~~~~~~~~~~~~~~~~~~~~~~~

An appeal: In Chapter 6, Bunyan includes a place of martyrs but indicates the hope of this becoming a passing reality. In our day, however, persecution is increasing to an alarming degree. Christians are suffering intensely in many parts of the world and are beginning to suffer here, too. Will you commit to add the persecuted Church to your prayer list?

~~~~~~~~~~~~~~~~~~~~~~~~~

~~~~~~~~~~~~~~~~~~~~~~~~~

Scriptures for Further Reflection

Matthew 5:10-12
Matthew 10:16-39
2 Timothy 3:10-13
2 Thessalonians 1:4-5
Isaiah 57:1-2
Psalm 119:19

~~~~~~~~~~~~~~~~~~~~~~~~~

NOTES:

_____

_____

_____

_____

_____

_____

_____

_____

_____

_____

_____

SCRIPTURES USED IN THIS CHAPTER

1 Peter 2:11 WEB
Beloved, I beg you as foreigners and pilgrims (in the world*), to abstain from fleshly lusts, which war against the soul. (*The NIV translations clarifies by adding "in the world".)

John 15:18-20
"If the world hates you, know that it has hated me before it hated you. ¹⁹If you were of the world, the world would love you as its own; but because you are not of the world, but I chose you out of the world, therefore the world hates

you. [20]Remember the word that I said to you: 'A servant is not greater than his master.' If they persecuted me, they will also persecute you. If they kept my word, they will also keep yours.

Revelation 3:11

I am coming soon. Hold fast what you have, so that no one may seize your crown.

1 Corinthians 9:24-27 WEB

Don't you know that those who run in a race all run, but one receives the prize? Run like that, that you may win. [25]Every man who strives in the games exercises self-control in all things. Now they do it to receive a corruptible crown, but we an incorruptible. [26]I therefore run like that, not aimlessly. I fight like that, not beating the air, [27]but I beat my body and bring it into submission, lest by any means, after I have preached to others, I myself should be rejected.

Isaiah 50:7

But the Lord GOD helps me; therefore I have not been disgraced; therefore I have set my face like a flint, and I know that I shall not be put to shame.

Philippians 3:13-16 NLT

. . . but I focus on this one thing: Forgetting the past and looking forward to what lies ahead, [14]I press on to reach the end of the race and receive the heavenly prize for which God, through Christ Jesus, is calling us. [15]Let all who are spiritually mature agree on these things. If you disagree on some point, I believe God will make it plain to you. [16]But we must hold on to the progress we have already made.

Matthew 4:1-11

Then Jesus was led up by the Spirit into the wilderness to be tempted by the devil. [2]And after fasting forty days and forty nights, he was hungry. [3]And the tempter came and said to him, "If you are the Son of God, command these stones to become loaves of bread." [4]But he answered, "It is written, 'Man shall not live by bread alone, but by every word that comes from the mouth of God.'" [5]Then the devil took him to the holy city and set him on the pinnacle of the temple [6]and said to him, "If you are the Son of God, throw yourself down, for it is written, 'He will command his angels concerning you,' and 'On their hands they will bear you up, lest you strike your foot against a stone.'" [7]Jesus said to him, "Again it is written, 'You shall not put the Lord your God to the test.'" [8]Again, the devil took him to a very high mountain and showed him all the kingdoms of the world and their glory. [9]And he said to him, "All these I will give you, if you will fall down and worship me." [10]Then Jesus said to him, "Be gone, Satan! For it is written, "'You shall worship the Lord your God and him only shall you serve.'" [11]Then the devil left him, and behold, angels came and were ministering to him.

Ephesians 2:1-9

And you were dead in the trespasses and sins [2]in which you once walked, following the course of this world, following the prince of the power of the air, the spirit that is now at work in the sons of disobedience— [3]among whom we all once lived in the passions of our flesh, carrying out the desires of the body and the mind, and were by nature children of wrath, like the rest of mankind. [4]But God, being rich in mercy, because of the great love with which he loved us, [5]even when we were dead in our trespasses, made us alive together with Christ—by grace you have been saved— [6]and raised us up with him and seated us with him in the heavenly places in Christ Jesus, [7]so that in the coming ages he might show the immeasurable riches of his grace in kindness toward us in Christ Jesus. [8]For by grace you have been saved through faith. And this is not your own doing; it is the gift of God, [9]not a result of works, so that no one may boast.

Mark 4:18-19

And others are the ones sown among thorns. They are those who hear the word, [19]but the cares of the world and the deceitfulness of riches and the desires for other things enter in and choke the word, and it proves unfruitful.

Proverbs 23:23

Buy truth, and do not sell it; buy wisdom, instruction, and understanding.

CHAPTER

10

~~~~~~~~~~~~~~~~~~~~~~~~~~~~

Progress Memory Verse

Don't love the world or the things that are in the world. If anyone loves the world, the Father's love isn't in him.

--1 John 2:15

~~~~~~~~~~~~~~~~~~~~~~~~~~~~

TO BEGIN

Did a Christian friend influence you to put your faith in Christ? How did that happen?

HOPEFUL JOINS CHRISTIAN

1. Christian didn't travel far before he had the joy of another pilgrim joining him. Who was he, and how did he decide to become a pilgrim? What wonderfully encouraging message did he bring?

2. A new pilgrim became "Hopeful" and left Vanity Fair after watching the example of Christian and Faithful. How can this story encourage us when we face growing hostility to the Christian faith? What does it tell you about how to respond to hatred?

3. What do the names Faithful and Hopeful tell you about these two pilgrims? How does this support the fact that we are uniquely gifted and that God does not expect us to be "cookie-cutter" Christians?

4. Name some people who have inspired faith and hope in you. How can you incorporate their attitudes and actions into your life?

5. How did Christian and Hopeful commit themselves to each other?

~~~~~~~~~~~~~~~~~~~~~~~~~~

Definition: Covenant

In our story, we see Christian and Hopeful enter into covenant with each other. A covenant is an agreement that lays out rights and responsibilities between individuals or groups. When people covenant together, they become obligated to their agreement. There are many covenants in the Bible, both between God and His people and between individuals. The most wonderful covenant for us is the one Jesus Christ made in His blood (Matthew 26:28). Historically, many churches have made covenants where members agree upon their duties toward God and fellow believers. The commitment Christian and Hopeful make to each other will help them through many trying times and will sustain them through their pilgrimage together.

~~~~~~~~~~~~~~~~~~~~~~~~~~

THE PILGRIMS MEET MR. BY-ENDS

6. The "fair" in the city of Fair-speech indicates that only courteous and agreeable words are spoken there. What is the error of Fair-speech?

7. (*) *By-end* literally means "a selfish motive." Let's choose definitions to match the other genteel citizens of Fair-speech. Put the definition letter in the space beside the name.

_____Lord Turn-about   A. To have a refined surface texture, pleasing to the senses

_____Lord Time-server   B. Giving a false appearance; pretending

_____Mr. Smooth-man   C. An opportunist who conforms his life and opinions to the prevailing culture of the times.

_____Mr. Facing-bothways   D. Two-faced, double-dealing, hypocritical

_____Mr. Any-thing   E. Changes direction without qualms

_____Rev. Two-tongues   F. Wants anything and everything this world offers

_____Lady Feigning   G. Makes contrary declarations on the same subject at different times; deceitful

MR. BY-ENDS'S RELIGION

8. Mr. By-ends and the citizens of Fair-speech are religious. In what two ways does Mr. By-ends claim that their religion differs from the "stricter sort" of faith?

   a.

   b.

9. The Fair-speech religion will always "go with the flow." Do you see this philosophy expressed in the Church today? In what ways is this dangerous to the Church's mission? What choices are you making to swim against the cultural current?

10. The Fair-speech religion is bold when it meets the sunshine of cultural approval. As you see storm clouds forming, how willing are you to head into the storm of disapproval?

THEY MUST PART COMPANY

11. What were Christian's reasons for telling Mr. By-ends that they could not be pilgrims together? How does Philippians 4:11-12 speak to this? Also, how do Amos 3:3 and 2 Corinthians 6:14-15 apply?

MR. BY-ENDS'S THREE FRIENDS

12. Our King made clear His highest purpose. How do His motives differ from those of Mr. By-ends and his friends? (See John 4:34, 5:30, 6:38, 8:29, 14:31, 17:4.)

THEY EVALUATE CHRISTIAN AND HOPEFUL

13. Mr. By-ends and his three friends talked about Christian and Hopeful. What were some of their criticisms?

14. Though the foursome thought they had Christian and Hopeful figured out, they did not. Why not, according to 1 Corinthians 2:14-15?

15. (*) The devil twisted Holy Scripture to use against Jesus, and so do those who embrace his doctrine. Mr. Hold-the-world twists specific Scriptures and also cites Abraham, Solomon, and Job to justify his position. How does he twist the following verses?

   Matthew 10:16

   Matthew 5:45

   Job 22:24

16. Scripture-twisting is dangerous. What does 2 Peter 3:15b-16 say about this?

A QUESTION FROM MR. BY-ENDS

17. Mr. By-ends proposes a question that Mr. Money-love answers and the four friends celebrate. To them, becoming religious for impure motives is quite sensible. They even view a minister who pleases others for personal advantage as wise, indeed. The Apostle Paul tried to please people, but his motive differed. How? (See 1 Corinthians 10:32-33.)

18. Why is it impossible to embrace the values of both God and the world? (See Luke 16:13.)

19. A self-centered, feel-good, "What's-in-it-for-me?" gospel seems rampant in our land. Examine your own heart for these sub-Christian motives. Is any of your Christian service done to please yourself or to impress others? Ask the Holy Spirit to enable you to serve purely from a heart of love for God and His glory. Write a personal prayer with this in mind:

CHRISTIAN ANSWERS THE QUESTION

20. How does Christian's use of Scripture differ from that of the worldly men of Fair-speech? What does this tell you about the value of solid teaching? Do you believe you can refute false teaching by using proper biblical interpretation? Do you recall the advice Paul gave in 2 Timothy 2:15?

21. What do you think a godly culture looks like? Can you think of ways God's people can do better at promoting a godly culture in their lives, homes, and world? Can you think of specifics you can apply in your home, church, and community?

~~~~~~~~~~~~~~~~~~~~~~~~~~

Scriptures for Further Reflection

Colossians 3:1-4
Romans 12:1-2
1 Corinthians 4:9-13
Matthew 23:27-28
Ephesians 5:6-11
Hosea 12:8
Luke 12:30-34

~~~~~~~~~~~~~~~~~~~~~~~~~~

NOTES:

_____

_____

_____

_____

_____

_____

_____

_____

_____

_____

_____

_____

_____

_____

_____

_____

_____

_____

_____

_____

_____

_____

_____

SCRIPTURES USED IN THIS CHAPTER

Philippians 4:11-12

Not that I am speaking of being in need, for I have learned in whatever situation I am to be content. [12]I know how to be brought low, and I know how to abound. In any and every circumstance, I have learned the secret of facing plenty and hunger, abundance and need.

Amos 3:3
"Do two walk together, unless they have agreed to meet?

2 Corinthians 6:14-15 NLT
Don't team up with those who are unbelievers. How can righteousness be a partner with wickedness? How can light live with darkness? ¹⁵What harmony can there be between Christ and the devil? How can a believer be a partner with an unbeliever?

John 4:34, 5:30, 6:38, 8:29, 14:31, 17:4
⁴:³⁴Jesus said to them, "My food is to do the will of him who sent me and to accomplish his work. ⁵:³⁰I can do nothing on my own. As I hear, I judge, and my judgment is just, because I seek not my own will but the will of him who sent me. ⁶:³⁸For I have come down from heaven, not to do my own will but the will of him who sent me. ⁸:²⁹And he who sent me is with me. He has not left me alone, for I always do the things that are pleasing to him." ¹⁴:³¹but I do as the Father has commanded me, so that the world may know that I love the Father. ¹⁷:⁴I glorified you on earth, having accomplished the work that you gave me to do.

1 Corinthians 2:14-15
The natural person does not accept the things of the Spirit of God, for they are folly to him, and he is not able to understand them because they are spiritually discerned. ¹⁵The spiritual person judges all things, but is himself to be judged by no one.

1 Corinthians 10:32-33
Give no offense to Jews or to Greeks or to the church of God, ³³just as I try to please everyone in everything I do, not seeking my own advantage, but that of many, that they may be saved.

Luke 16:13
No servant can serve two masters, for either he will hate the one and love the other, or he will be devoted to the one and despise the other. You cannot serve God and money.

Matthew 10:16
Behold, I am sending you out as sheep in the midst of wolves, so be wise as serpents and innocent as doves.

Matthew 5:45 NLT
In that way, you will be acting as true children of your Father in heaven. For he gives his sunlight to both the evil and the good, and he sends rain on the just and the unjust alike.

Job 22:24 (in context, 23-25)
If you return to the Almighty you will be built up; if you remove injustice far from your tents, ²⁴if you lay gold in the dust, and gold of Ophir among the stones of the torrent bed, ²⁵then the Almighty will be your gold and your precious silver.

2 Peter 3:15b-16 NLT
This is what our beloved brother Paul also wrote to you with the wisdom God gave him — ¹⁶speaking of these things in all of his letters. Some of his comments are hard to understand, and those who are ignorant and unstable have twisted his letters to mean something quite different, just as they do with other parts of Scripture. And this will result in their destruction.

2 Timothy 2:15
Do your best to present yourself to God as one approved, a worker who has no need to be ashamed, rightly handling the word of truth.

CHAPTER

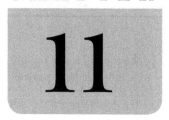

~~~~~~~~~~~~~~~~~~~~~~~~~~

Progress Memory Verse

But I will hope continually and will praise you yet more and more. My mouth will tell of your righteous acts, of your deeds of salvation all the day, for their number is past my knowledge.

--Psalm 71:14-15

~~~~~~~~~~~~~~~~~~~~~~~~~~

TO BEGIN

Have you ever made a joyful escape from a situation you thought might undo you? Explain.

IN THE PLAIN CALLED EASE

1. Lucre means "illicit gain." The attraction to this is found several places in the Bible. Who are the pcoplc in 1 Samuel 8:3, Judges 16:5, 18; 2 Kings 5:20-27; Esther 3:8-9; Matthew 26:14-16? What did they have in common?

2. Sometimes the Lord allows us a short period of respite like the plain called "Ease." But enjoying a state of ease also brings dangers. Why do you think a silver-mine like "Lucre" would be found in this place?

3. A number of times, the New Testament addresses the "lucre" issue in reference to church leadership. (See 1 Timothy 3:3, 8; Titus 1:7, 11; 1 Peter 5:2, KJV.) How do you see this as a concern for leaders and their flocks?

THE APPEAL OF DEMAS

4. Read Colossians 4:14 and Philemon 23-24. What two Early Church men are common to both passages? Which of them deserted the Apostle Paul, and what was his downfall (see 2 Timothy 4:9-10)? The other authored two New Testament books and never abandoned the Apostle Paul. Who was he (see 2 Timothy 4:11)? How does this make you feel about the kind of legacy you want to leave?

5. Double-minded religion—especially that which seeks to unite love of money with a true pilgrimage—does not end well. What happened to By-ends and his friends? How does Jesus warn us in Matthew 16:26?

THE PILLAR OF LOT'S WIFE

6. When the two pilgrims discussed Lot's wife, how did they think her example could be useful in the future?

THE RIVER OF GOD

7. The pilgrims resisted the temptations of Lucre. What special blessing did the Holy Spirit bestow after that victory? Why might this blessing follow?

8. Do you need refreshment in the Holy Spirit? What does Jesus promise you in Luke 11:13 and in John 7:37-39? Write a statement here that expresses your heart – asking, believing, receiving, and thanking God for allowing you to drink of the "River of Life." Spend some time waiting on Him -- positively reflecting on Him and resting in His goodness. Record any blessing you receive from this time:

TEMPTATION TO LEAVE THE ROUGH WAY

9. After the pilgrim's had a blessed experience at the River of God, what happened that made them "very sorry"? Why did this make them sorry?

10. How did Christian's temptation to leave the Way progress in his heart?

~~~~~~

Progress Quotes from Other Pilgrims

The nature of the enemy's warfare in your life is to cause you to become discouraged and to cast away your confidence. Not that you would necessarily discard your salvation, but you could give up your hope of God's deliverance. The enemy wants to numb you into a coping kind of Christianity that has given up hope of seeing God's resurrection power.

— Bob Sorge, *Glory: When Heaven Invades Earth*

Doubt discovers difficulties which it never solves; it creates hesitancy, despondency, despair. Its progress is the decay of comfort, the death of peace. "Believe!" is the word which speaks life into a man, but doubt nails down his coffin.

— Charles Spurgeon

~~~~~~

11. (*) After enjoying profoundly satisfying experiences in the Holy Spirit, we may be tempted to think that our troubles are behind us. Jesus experienced a profound encounter with the Spirit but endured intense temptations directly following it. What was His spiritual experience? (See Matthew 3:15-17.) We looked at His temptation in Ch. 9 of our study, but let's look at it again. How did Jesus fight the temptations? (See Matthew 3:16-4:11.)

12. (*) Christian and Hopeful thought their pilgrimage had gotten too difficult. The disciplines and responsibilities seemed too taxing. They neglected some important things that would have helped them with their attitude and perspective. What do you think they were, and how can you avoid similar errors in judgment?

BY-PATH MEADOW

13. Once the pilgrims went into Bypath Meadow, whom did they see and choose to follow? What became of this person?

~~~~~~~~~~~~~~~~~~~~~~~~~

Progress Tip

God never promised a smooth and easy pilgrimage. When we turn from His Way – trusting our own will and wisdom to make things better – trouble will follow.

Hopefully, you will always have the sense to stay away from places like Bypath Meadow. If, however, you do find yourself in such a gloomy place, you should remember that Doubting Castle and Giant Despair experiences are never God's will for you. Rather, He always offers grace, deliverance from bondage, and restoration. Remember His love, and trust His promises. They will not fail you.

~~~~~~~~~~~~~~~~~~~~~~~~~

14. Think about the presumptuous confidence of the man named Vain-Confidence. In our darkening world, how do you think this character can serve as a warning? Also, the younger pilgrim followed the older one into danger. What should this tell you about your responsibility toward your own soul? (See 1 John 3:7.)

15. The pilgrims heard the Spirit's encouraging voice telling them to turn back to the Highway. But they failed in their effort. What kind of emotions can make it especially hard to find our way back after falling into sin?

SEIZED BY GIANT DESPAIR

16. What a foolish decision the pilgrims made when they opted to postpone returning to the Way. What happened in the morning, and why did this take place?

DISTRUST'S PERSUASIONS

17. What is the name of Giant Despair's wife? What is her influence? How can distrust be a powerful influence against our own pilgrimage?

~~~~~~~~~~~~~~~~~~~~~~~~

Definition: Hope

For the Christian, hope is a confident expectation based on the guarantees of God's Word. This hope has nothing in common with wishful thinking, which has no guarantee. Biblical hope is a *know-so*; not a *hope-so*. For example, the Bible calls our expectation of Christ's Second Coming "The Blessed Hope." (See Titus 2:13.) We also live by hope, putting on *the hope of salvation as a helmet* (1Thessalonians 5:8b). God's Word even urges us to *be joyful in hope* (Romans 12:12a). Granted, we may go through severe trials; however, God's people always possess a sure hope in Christ. *And hope does not disappoint us* (Romans 5:5).

~~~~~~~~~~~~~~~~~~~~~~~~

HOPEFUL REFUSES TO ABANDON ALL HOPE

18. In his deep depression, Christian only sees two options. What are they? How does Hopeful help him with his thinking?

19. (*) When David committed adultery with Bathsheba and conspired against her husband, he ventured into a Bypath Meadow. Confronted with his sin, he felt great remorse and landed in his own Dungeon of Despair. This resulted in Psalm 51. Take a few minutes to read this prayer. Can you identify with his pain? Pray through this psalm and record a few parts that you find meaningful.

REMEMBERING THE KEY OF PROMISE

20. Christian remembered the Key in his pocket to unlock the dungeon. What does this key represent? Why do you think it's easy to forget this key?

ESCAPE FROM DOUBTING CASTLE

21. What had the pilgrims done that night that sparked the revelation that brought about their escape?

22. Have you ever suffered with feelings of doubt, fear, or despair and finally rediscovered the joy of God's grace by using a "key of promise"? Do you need that right now? Write a prayer that uses one of your "keys of promise."

~~~~~~~~~~~~~~~~~~~~~~~~

Key Pilgrim's Perspective

The world soothes itself with false hopes. But like a vicious giant, "Despair" will ultimately seize and destroy every unbeliever's soul. Christians, on the other hand, should never allow this giant to bully them. We are people of genuine hope, not despair. Still, getting into Doubting Castle is so incredibly easy. Any conviction of sin without a corresponding hope in Christ's mercy can drive Christian pilgrims there. In this condition, we can actually think the giant has some legal right to march us into his dungeon. But that is a lie! If we truly repent of our sins, that miraculous key always is available for opening every prison door.

~~~~~~~~~~~~~~~~~~~~~~~~

23. What was the first thing the two pilgrims did upon returning to the King's Highway?

24. Think of yourself as a Hopeful in this world. How will you advise those imprisoned in despair?

"Blessed Be Your Name" (Matt Redman)

Blessed Be Your Name
In the land that is plentiful
Where Your streams of abundance flow
Blessed be Your name

Blessed Be Your name
When I'm found in the desert place
Though I walk through the wilderness
Blessed Be Your name

Every blessing You pour out
I'll turn back to praise
When the darkness closes in, Lord
Still I will say

Blessed be Your name
When the sun's shining down on me
When the world's 'all as it should be'
Blessed be Your name

Blessed be Your name
On the road marked with suffering
Though there's pain in the offering
Blessed be Your name

Every blessing You pour out
I'll turn back to praise
When the darkness closes in, Lord
Still I will say

Blessed be the name of the Lord
Blessed be Your name
Blessed be the name of the Lord
Blessed be Your glorious name

You give and take away
You give and take away
My heart will choose to say
Lord, blessed be Your name

~~~~~~~~~~~~~~~~~~~~~~~~

Scriptures for Further Reflection

Psalm 119:14, 72
Proverbs 19:27
Romans 5:2-5
Romans 8:24-25
Psalm 33:18-22
Romans 4:18-22
Mark 11:22-24
Isaiah 49:13-16

~~~~~~~~~~~~~~~~~~~~~~~~

NOTES:

_____

_____

_____

_____

_____

_____

_____

_____

_____

_____

_____

_____

_____

_____

_____

_____

_____

_____

_____

_____

_____

_____

SCRIPTURES USED IN THIS CHAPTER

1 Samuel 8:1-3

When Samuel became old, he made his sons judges over Israel. [2]The name of his firstborn son was Joel, and the name of his second, Abijah; they were judges in Beersheba. [3]Yet his sons did not walk in his ways but turned aside after gain. They took bribes and perverted justice.

Judges 16:5, 18

[5]And the lords of the Philistines came up to her and said to her, "Seduce him, and see where his great strength lies, and by what means we may overpower him, that we may bind him to humble him. And we will each give you 1,100 pieces of silver." [18]When Delilah saw that he had told her all his heart, she sent and called the lords of the Philistines, saying, "Come up again, for he has told me all his heart." Then the lords of the Philistines came up to her and brought the money in their hands.

2 Kings 5:20-27

Gehazi, the servant of Elisha the man of God, said, "See, my master has spared this Naaman the Syrian, in not accepting from his hand what he brought. As the LORD lives, I will run after him and get something from him." [21]So Gehazi followed Naaman. And when Naaman saw someone running after him, he got down from the chariot to meet him and said, "Is all well?" [22]And he said, "All is well. My master has sent me to say, 'There have just now come to me from the hill country of Ephraim two young men of the sons of the prophets. Please give them a talent of silver and two festal garments.'" [23]And Naaman said, "Be pleased to accept two talents." And he urged him and tied up two talents of silver in two bags, with two festal garments, and laid them on two of his servants. And they carried them before Gehazi. [24]And when he came to the hill, he took them from their hand and put them in the house, and he sent the men away, and they departed. [25]He went in and stood before his master, and Elisha said to him, "Where have you been, Gehazi?" And he said, "Your servant went nowhere." [26]But he said to him, "Did not my heart go when the man turned from his chariot to meet you? Was it a time to accept money and garments, olive orchards and vineyards, sheep and oxen, male servants and female servants? [27]Therefore the leprosy of Naaman shall cling to you and to your descendants forever." So he went out from his presence a leper, like snow.

Esther 3:8-9

Then Haman said to King Ahasuerus, "There is a certain people scattered abroad and dispersed among the peoples in all the provinces of your kingdom. Their laws are different from those of every other people, and they do not keep the king's laws, so that it is not to the king's profit to tolerate them. [9]If it please the king, let it be decreed that they be destroyed, and I will pay 10,000 talents of silver into the hands of those who have charge of the king's business, that they may put it into the king's treasuries."

Matthew 26:14-16

Then one of the twelve, whose name was Judas Iscariot, went to the chief priests [15]and said, "What will you give me if I deliver him over to you?" And they paid him thirty pieces of silver. [16]And from that moment he sought an opportunity to betray him.

1 Timothy 3:3, 8 (KJV)

[3]Not given to wine, no striker, not greedy of filthy lucre; but patient, not a brawler, not covetous [8]Likewise must the deacons be grave, not double-tongued, not given to much wine, not greedy of filthy lucre.

Titus 1:7, 11 KJV

[7]For a bishop must be blameless, as the steward of God; not self-willed, not soon angry, not given to wine, no striker, not given to filthy lucre; [11]Whose mouths must be stopped, who subvert whole houses, teaching things which they ought not, for filthy lucre's sake.

1 Peter 5:2 KJV

Feed the flock of God which is among you, taking the oversight thereof, not by constraint, but willingly; not for filthy lucre, but of a ready mind.

Colossians 4:14

Luke the beloved physician greets you, as does Demas.

Philemon 23-24

Epaphras, my fellow prisoner in Christ Jesus, sends greetings to you, [24]and so do Mark, Aristarchus, Demas, and Luke, my fellow workers.

2 Timothy 4:9-11

Do your best to come to me soon. [10]For Demas, in love with this present world, has deserted me and gone to Thessalonica. Crescens has gone to Galatia, Titus to Dalmatia. [11]Luke alone is with me. . .

Matthew 16:26 NLT

And what do you benefit if you gain the whole world but lose your own soul? Is anything worth more than your soul?

Luke 11:13

If you then, who are evil, know how to give good gifts to your children, how much more will the heavenly Father give the Holy Spirit to those who ask him!

John 7:37-39

On the last day of the feast, the great day, Jesus stood up and cried out, "If anyone thirsts, let him come to me and drink. [38]Whoever believes in me, as the Scripture has said, 'Out of his heart will flow rivers of living water.'" [39]Now this he said about the Spirit, whom those who believed in him were to receive, for as yet the Spirit had not been given, because Jesus was not yet glorified.

Matthew 3:15-17; 3:16-4:11

[3:15]But Jesus answered him, "Let it be so now, for thus it is fitting for us to fulfill all righteousness." Then he consented. [16]And when Jesus was baptized, immediately he went up from the water, and behold, the heavens were opened to him, and he saw the Spirit of God descending like a dove and coming to rest on him; [17]and behold, a voice from heaven said, "This is my beloved Son, with whom I am well pleased." [4:1]Then Jesus was led up by the Spirit into the wilderness to be tempted by the devil. [2]And after fasting forty days and forty nights, he was hungry. [3]And the tempter came and said to him, "If you are the Son of God, command these stones to become loaves of bread." [4]But he answered, "It is written, 'Man shall not live by bread alone, but by every word that comes from the mouth of God.'" [5]Then the devil took him to the holy city and set him on the pinnacle of the temple [6]and said to him, "If you are the Son of God, throw yourself down, for it is written, 'He will command his angels concerning you,' and 'On their hands they will bear you up, lest you strike your foot against a stone.'" [7]Jesus said to him, "Again it is written, 'You shall not put the Lord your God to the test.'" [8]Again, the devil took him to a very high mountain and showed him all the kingdoms of the world and their glory. [9]And he said to him, "All these I will give you, if you will fall down and worship me." [10]Then Jesus said to him, "Be gone, Satan! For it is written, 'You shall worship the Lord your God and him only shall you serve.'" [11]Then the devil left him, and behold, angels came and were ministering to him.

1 John 3:7

Little children, let no one deceive you. Whoever practices righteousness is righteous, as he is righteous.

Psalm 51

Have mercy on me, O God, according to your steadfast love; according to your abundant mercy blot out my transgressions. [2]Wash me thoroughly from my iniquity, and cleanse me from my sin! [3]For I know my transgressions, and my sin is ever before me. [4]Against you, you only, have I sinned and done what is evil in your sight, so that you may be justified in your words and blameless in your judgment. [5]Behold, I was brought forth in iniquity, and in sin did my mother conceive me. [6]Behold, you delight in truth in the inward being, and you teach me wisdom in the secret heart. [7]Purge me with hyssop, and I shall be clean; wash me, and I shall be whiter than snow. [8]Let me hear joy and gladness; let the bones that you have broken rejoice. [9]Hide your face from my sins, and blot out all my iniquities. [10]Create in me a clean heart, O God, and renew a right spirit within me. [11]Cast me not away from your presence, and take not your Holy Spirit from me. [12]Restore to me the joy of your salvation, and uphold me with a willing spirit. [13]Then I will teach transgressors your ways, and sinners will return to you. [14]Deliver me from bloodguiltiness, O God, O God of my salvation, and my tongue will sing aloud of your righteousness. [15]O Lord, open my lips, and my mouth will declare your praise. [16]For you will not delight in sacrifice, or I would give it; you will not be pleased with a burnt offering. [17]The sacrifices of God are a broken spirit; a broken and contrite heart, O God, you will not despise. [18]Do good to Zion in your good pleasure; build up the walls of Jerusalem; [19]then will you delight in right sacrifices, in burnt offerings and whole burnt offerings; then bulls will be offered on your altar.

1Timothy 6:3-11

If anyone teaches a different doctrine and does not agree with the sound words of our Lord Jesus Christ and the teaching that accords with godliness, [4]he is puffed up with conceit and understands nothing. He has an unhealthy craving for controversy and for quarrels about words, which produce envy, dissension, slander, evil suspicions, [5]and constant friction among people who are depraved in mind and deprived of the truth, imagining that godliness is a means of gain. [6]Now there is great gain in godliness with contentment, [7]for we brought nothing into the world, and we cannot take anything out of the world. [8]But if we have food and clothing, with these we will be content. [9]But those who desire to be rich fall into temptation, into a snare, into many senseless and harmful desires that plunge people into ruin and destruction. [10]For the love of money is a root of all kinds of evils. It is through this craving that some have wandered away from the faith and pierced themselves with many pangs. [11]But as for you, O man of God, flee these things. Pursue righteousness, godliness, faith, love, steadfastness, gentleness.

CHAPTER

12

~~~~~~~~~~~~~~~~~~~~~~~~~~~~~~~

Progress Memory Verse

Dear brothers and sisters, honor those who are your leaders in the Lord's work. They work hard among you and give you spiritual guidance. Show them great respect and wholehearted love because of their work. And live peacefully with each other.

--1 Thessalonians 5:12-13 NLT

~~~~~~~~~~~~~~~~~~~~~~~~~~~~~~~

TO BEGIN

Have you ever had an insight or experience that gave you a fresh perspective of heaven's glory? Can you describe it?

THE DELECTABLE MOUNTAINS

1. What were the Shepherds doing when Christian and Faithful approached them? If the Shepherds represent pastors, how does their activity relate to a pastor's task? What did Jesus repeatedly emphasize that Peter do in John 21:15-17?

2. Early in his pilgrimage, Christian glimpsed the Delectable Mountains from the Palace Beautiful. Despite the ups and downs of his experience, he now finds himself here. How does this encourage you in your own progress?

~~~~~~~~~~~~~~~~~~~~~~~~~

Note:

Commentators have interpreted the Delectable Mountains to mean many things: a time of rest and reflection after a terrible trial; the local church, equipped with faithful pastors; the richness of observing the Lord's Day; a "mountaintop experience" found in resting, reflecting, and receiving sound instruction.

~~~~~~~~~~~~~~~~~~~~~~~~~

3. When the pilgrims asked the Shepherds about whose sheep they were feeding, what did the Shepherds reply? Why is this noteworthy? What instruction and promise does the Apostle Peter give leaders in 1 Peter 5:1-4?

4. What do you think the names of the Shepherds indicate about the spiritual attributes desired in a shepherd over God's flock? Be sure to refer to the Scriptures provided:

a. Knowledge (2 Timothy 3:14-17)

b. Experience (Job 12:12-13, 1 Timothy 3:6)

c. Watchful (Acts 20:28-32)

d. Sincere (2 Timothy 1:5, 1 Timothy 1:3-7, 1 Peter 1:22)

~~~~~~~~~~~~~~~~~~~~~~~~~

Key Pilgrim's Perspective

The four Shepherds represent the role of pastors. The New Testament uses the Greek word for shepherd, poimen, metaphorically of Christian pastors. Like all shepherds, these four feed their flocks and tend them. Their names describe essential qualities of effective spiritual leaders. Too often, the Church looks more at charisma, eloquence, and credentials and then suffers for it. We need leaders who look to Jesus Christ, our Good Shepherd, as their leadership model. Leaders who protect their flocks from attack, who heal wounded and sick sheep, who rescue lost or trapped sheep, and who love and feed the sheep are jewels. We should pray for God to raise up more leaders who are spiritually knowledgeable, experienced, watchful, and sincere. We should esteem God's shepherds very highly.

~~~~~~~~~~~~~~~~~~~~~~~~~

5. The Shepherds were hospitable. What does Scripture command concerning this virtue in Christian leaders? (See 1 Timothy 3:2.) What is expected of the Church? (See Hebrews 13:2.)

A MOUNTAIN CALLED ERROR

~~~~~~~~~~~~~~~~~~~~~~~

Progress Quote from Another Pilgrim

If sheep do not have the constant care of a shepherd, they will go the wrong way, unaware of the dangers at hand. They have been known to nibble themselves right off the side of a mountain. And so, because sheep are sheep, they need shepherds to care for them.

--Kay Arthur

~~~~~~~~~~~~~~~~~~~~~~~

6. The Shepherds showed the pilgrims some "wonders." The first place was a mountain called Error from which Hymenacus and Philetus had fallen. What advice does Paul give his protégé Timothy, and how did these two men illustrate his point? (See 2 Timothy 2:15-18.)

7. Why does Paul feel so urgent about Christian leaders teaching "sound doctrine"? (See Titus 1:7a, 9-11; 2 Timothy 4:1-4.)

8. How does standing on the edge of a doctrinal cliff make you feel? Can you think of some dangerous doctrines or teachings you have heard in our day? How can you assure your safety from their perils?

A MOUNTAIN CALLED CAUTION

~~~~~~~~~~~~~~~~~~~~~~~~~

Definition: Caution

Caution, meaning watchful forethought to avoid danger
or evil, is a trait of great value to a Christian pilgrimage.
When we exercise caution, we give careful attention and
vigilance to minimizing our risk in hazardous places. In
Matthew 24, Jesus warns of terrible times in the future
when believers will need to journey forward with utmost
caution.

~~~~~~~~~~~~~~~~~~~~~~~~~

9. The Shepherds next took the pilgrims to the Mountain called Caution where they are reminded of
their own close call. What warning from Proverbs 21:16 did one Shepherd give? Also, the pilgrims
had followed Vain-confidence into deeper trouble. How does Proverbs 13:20 speak to this danger?

Proverbs 21:16:

Proverbs 13:20:

10. (*) A stubborn religious spirit also ignores caution. Jesus had little tolerance for this condition. What
did He call the religious leaders who refused to hear Him? (See Matthew 23:16, 17, 19, 24, 26.)
According to Matthew 15:14, what made these men so dangerous?

11. (*) Paul expressed dismay at the Galatian church. (See Galatians 3:1.) What happened to their
spiritual eyesight? How does Peter advise believers to keep their spiritual eyesight sharp, and what
does he imply about the result of not taking this admonition seriously? (See 2 Peter 1:5-11.)

12. How do the blind people among the tombs speak to you about using good judgment and taking the
Holy Spirit's guidance more seriously?

A BY-WAY TO HELL

13. Why do you think the Shepherds took the pilgrims to the By-way to Hell and had them look inside?

14. Speaking about Hell has become unpopular for preachers today, yet it is a significant part of the truth. Even the lovely Delectable Mountains have a passage to Hell for hypocrites. How does Jesus address hypocrites in Matthew 23:33? What "caution" does He give in Luke 12:1, and what implication can you see in His analogy?

15. What are some of the instructions and warnings that Paul gives in 2 Corinthians 13:5 and Colossians 2:6-8?

16. We do our best, walking humbly and diligently before God. But He alone provides the grace and mercy to see us through to the end. How does Jude 1:24 encourage you?

A VIEW OF THE CITY

~~~~~~~~~~~~~~~~~~~~~~~~~

Progress Tip

Come to the Delectable Mountains. Take time to nourish your souls with the rich provision found there. Make a serious pursuit of learning from godly shepherds. Their guidance will help keep you from danger and train your spiritual eyes, and with their support, you may even see glimpses of heaven.

~~~~~~~~~~~~~~~~~~~~~~~~~

17. Praise God! The Shepherds don't leave the pilgrims buried in fear and caution after all. What was the high hill they climbed? What did they need to see clearly? What hindered them?

18. Perhaps they cannot yet see clearly, but the pilgrims remember how near they had come to complete blindness. And now they actually get to glimpse heaven's glory! How does this scene and also Paul's words in 1 Corinthians 13:12 encourage you?

19. This world tends to keep us focused on the earthly realm. Thus, it's not always easy to see from a heavenly perspective. The two pilgrims lacked skill to see clearly through the perspective glass. How do you think you can hone your skill? According to 1 Corinthians 2:9-12, who will help you perceive the heavenly things God has given you? What encourages you most about this passage of Scripture?

20. As any good pastors will do, the Shepherds send the pilgrims back into the world with instructions for their pilgrimage. How does Hebrews 13:17 say we should relate to our spiritual leaders?

~~~~~~~~~~~~~~~~~~~~~~~~~~~

Scriptures for Further Reflection

Isaiah 58:6-8
1 Samuel 16:6-7
2 John 9-11
2 Corinthians 11:3-4
Psalm 26:2-3
John 21:15-17
Jeremiah 3:15, 23:4
2 Peter 3:13-14

~~~~~~~~~~~~~~~~~~~~~~~~~~~

NOTES:

SCRIPTURES USED IN THIS CHAPTER

John 21:15-17

When they had finished breakfast, Jesus said to Simon Peter, "Simon, son of John, do you love me more than these?" He said to him, "Yes, Lord; you know that I love you." He said to him, "Feed my lambs." [16]He said to him a second time, "Simon, son of John, do you love me?" He said to him, "Yes, Lord; you know that I love you." He said to him, "Tend my sheep." [17]He said to him the third time, "Simon, son of John, do you love me?" Peter was grieved because he said to him the third time, "Do you love me?" and he said to him, "Lord, you know everything; you know that I love you." Jesus said to him, "Feed my sheep.

1 Peter 5:1-4

So I exhort the elders among you, as a fellow elder and a witness of the sufferings of Christ, as well as a partaker in the glory that is going to be revealed: [2]shepherd the flock of God that is among you, exercising oversight, not under compulsion, but willingly, as God would have you; not for shameful gain, but eagerly; [3]not domineering over those in your charge, but being examples to the flock. [4]And when the chief Shepherd appears, you will receive the unfading crown of glory.

2 Timothy 3:14-17

But as for you, continue in what you have learned and have firmly believed, knowing from whom you learned it [15]and how from childhood you have been acquainted with the sacred writings, which are able to make you wise for salvation through faith in Christ Jesus. [16]All Scripture is breathed out by God and profitable for teaching, for reproof, for correction, and for training in righteousness, [17]that the man of God may be competent, equipped for every good work.

Job 12:12-13

Wisdom is with the aged, and understanding in length of days. [13]"With God are wisdom and might; he has counsel and understanding.

1 Timothy 3:6

(An overseer) must not be a recent convert, or he may become puffed up with conceit and fall into the condemnation of the devil.

Acts 20:28-32

Pay careful attention to yourselves and to all the flock, in which the Holy Spirit has made you overseers, to care for the church of God, which he obtained with his own blood. [29]I know that after my departure fierce wolves will come in among you, not sparing the flock;[30]and from among your own selves will arise men speaking twisted things, to draw away the disciples after them.[31]Therefore be alert, remembering that for three years I did not cease night or day to admonish everyone with tears. [32]And now I commend you to God and to the word of his grace, which is able to build you up and to give you the inheritance among all those who are sanctified.

2 Timothy 1:5

I am reminded of your sincere faith, a faith that dwelt first in your grandmother Lois and your mother Eunice and now, I am sure, dwells in you as well.

1 Timothy 1:3-7

As I urged you when I was going to Macedonia, remain at Ephesus that you may charge certain persons not to teach any different doctrine, [4]nor to devote themselves to myths and endless genealogies, which promote speculations rather than the stewardship from God that is by faith. [5]The aim of our charge is love that issues from a pure heart and a good conscience and a sincere faith. [6]Certain persons, by swerving from these, have wandered away into vain discussion, [7]desiring to be teachers of the law, without understanding either what they are saying or the things about which they make confident assertions.

1 Peter 1:22

Having purified your souls by your obedience to the truth for a sincere brotherly love, love one another earnestly from a pure heart.

1 Timothy 3:2

Therefore an overseer must be above reproach, the husband of one wife, sober-minded, self-controlled, respectable, hospitable, able to teach.

Hebrews 13:2

Do not neglect to show hospitality to strangers, for thereby some have entertained angels unawares.

2 Timothy 2:15-18

Do your best to present yourself to God as one approved, a worker who has no need to be ashamed, rightly handling the word of truth. [16]But avoid irreverent babble, for it will lead people into more and more ungodliness, [17]and their talk will spread like gangrene. Among them are Hymenaeus and Philetus, [18]who have swerved from the truth, saying that the resurrection has already happened. They are upsetting the faith of some.

Titus 1:7a, 9-11 NIV

Since an overseer is entrusted with God's work, he must be blameless. . . . [9]He must hold firmly to the trustworthy message as it has been taught, so that he can encourage others by sound doctrine and refute those who oppose it. [10]For there are many rebellious people, mere talkers and deceivers, especially those of the circumcision group. [11]They must be silenced, because they are ruining whole households by teaching things they ought not to teach—and that for the sake of dishonest gain.

2 Timothy 4:1-4

I charge you in the presence of God and of Christ Jesus, who is to judge the living and the dead, and by his appearing and his kingdom: [2]preach the word; be ready in season and out of season; reprove, rebuke, and exhort, with complete patience and teaching. [3]For the time is coming when people will not endure sound teaching, but having itching ears they will accumulate for themselves teachers to suit their own passions, [4]and will turn away from listening to the truth and wander off into myths.

Proverbs 21:16 NIV

A man who strays from the path of understanding comes to rest in the company of the dead.

Proverbs 13:20

Whoever walks with the wise becomes wise, but the companion of fools will suffer harm.

Matthew 23:16-17, 19, 24, 26

Woe to you, blind guides, who say, "If anyone swears by the temple, it is nothing, but if anyone swears by the gold of the temple, he is bound by his oath." [17]You blind fools! For which is greater, the gold or the temple that has made the gold sacred? [19]You blind men! For which is greater, the gift or the altar that makes the gift sacred? [24]You blind guides, straining out a gnat and swallowing a camel! [26]You blind Pharisee! First clean the inside of the cup and the plate, that the outside also may be clean.

Matthew 15:14

Leave them alone. They are blind guides of the blind. If the blind guide the blind, both will fall into a pit."

Galatians 3:1 NIV

You foolish Galatians! Who has bewitched you? Before your very eyes Jesus Christ was clearly portrayed as crucified.

2 Peter 1:5-11

For this very reason, make every effort to supplement your faith with virtue, and virtue with knowledge, [6]and knowledge with self-control, and self-control with steadfastness, and steadfastness with godliness, [7]and godliness with brotherly affection, and brotherly affection with love. [8]For if these qualities are yours and are increasing, they keep you from being ineffective or unfruitful in the knowledge of our Lord Jesus Christ. [9]For whoever lacks these qualities is so nearsighted that he is blind, having forgotten that he was cleansed from his former sins. [10]Therefore, brothers, be all the more diligent to make your calling and election sure, for if you practice these qualities you will never fall. [11]For in this way there will be richly provided for you an entrance into the eternal kingdom of our Lord and Savior Jesus Christ. (ESV)

Matthew 23:33

You serpents, you brood of vipers, how are you to escape being sentenced to hell?

Luke 12:1 NIV

Meanwhile, when a crowd of many thousands had gathered, so that they were trampling on one another, Jesus began to speak first to his disciples, saying: "Be on your guard against the yeast of the Pharisees, which is hypocrisy.

2 Corinthians 13:5

Examine yourselves, to see whether you are in the faith. Test yourselves. Or do you not realize this about yourselves, that Jesus Christ is in you? —unless indeed you fail to meet the test!

Colossians 2:6-8

Therefore, as you received Christ Jesus the Lord, so walk in him, [7]rooted and built up in him and established in the faith, just as you were taught, abounding in thanksgiving. [8]See to it that no one takes you captive by philosophy and empty deceit, according to human tradition, according to the elemental spirits of the world, and not according to Christ.

Jude 1:24

Now to him who is able to keep you from stumbling, and to present you faultless before the presence of his glory in great joy, [25] to God our Savior, who alone is wise, be glory and majesty, dominion and power, both now and forever. Amen.

1 Corinthians 13:12 KJV

For now we see through a glass, darkly; but then face to face: now I know in part; but then shall I know even as also I am known.

1 Corinthians 2:9-12

But, as it is written, "What no eye has seen, nor ear heard, nor the heart of man imagined, what God has prepared for those who love him"— [10]these things God has revealed to us through the Spirit. For the Spirit searches everything, even the depths of God. [11]For who knows a person's thoughts except the spirit of that person, which is in him? So also no one comprehends the thoughts of God except the Spirit of God. [12]Now we have received not the spirit of the world, but the Spirit who is from God, that we might understand the things freely given us by God.

Hebrews 13:17

Obey your leaders and submit to them, for they are keeping watch over your souls, as those who will have to give an account. Let them do this with joy and not with groaning, for that would be of no advantage to you.

CHAPTER

~~~~~~~~~~~~~~~~~~~~~~~~~

Progress Memory Verse

But you, beloved, keep building up yourselves on your most holy faith, praying in the Holy Spirit. Keep yourselves in God's love, looking for the mercy of our Lord Jesus Christ to eternal life.

--Jude 1:20-21

~~~~~~~~~~~~~~~~~~~~~~~~~

TO BEGIN

Do you have an easier time relating with those who think more highly or more lowly of themselves? Explain.

WALKING WITH IGNORANCE

1. What do the name "Ignorance" and his residence, the "Country of Conceit," betray about the young man?

2. (*) In Romans 11, Paul explains to Gentile believers that God has graciously grafted them into His "olive tree." In verse 25, what does he seek to convey related to conceit?

3. In Luke 18:9-14, Jesus tells a parable about a Pharisee and a tax-collector. How is Ignorance like this Pharisee?

4. Have you ever visited the Country of Conceit? Do you still sometimes breathe its air? How do you resolve this? Write a prayer that expresses your heart.

Definition: Apostasy

Apostasy means to abandon one's faith or fall away. This word in Greek is *apostasia*. It is formed by two shorter words, *apo* "away from" and *stasis* "rebellion." It is also related to the word *apostasion*, meaning "divorce" and *aphistanai* "to revolt." Clearly, it marks a very serious spiritual condition. In Acts 21:21, Jews accused Paul of apostasy against Old Testament teachings when they accused him of forsaking Moses. In 1 Timothy 4:1, Paul predicts perilous times at the end of days that include a sizable apostasy from the Christian faith.

A MAN BEING CARRIED AWAY

5. Turn-away is quite different from Ignorance. He felt no need at all to be good. He lived a self-indulgent life, presumed upon God's grace, and fell into apostasy. Seven demons, therefore, had bound Turn-Away and carried him toward Hell. How do Matthew 12:43-45 and James 1:14-15 warn us?

6. At one point, Turn-away may have appeared to possess true faith. He certainly does not now, however. Look at Proverbs 4:23, 22:5, 23:19, and 28:26. What do Scriptures like these convey to you?

THE STORY OF LITTLE-FAITH

7. One thing led to another with Little-faith. Because of his carelessness and weak faith, he was unable to claim the Gospel's provision of grace when needed. What three villains pounced on him, and what did they steal?

8. If the jewels represent the Spirit's graces that unite one's soul to Christ, what might the spending money represent?

9. Why did Little-faith continue to live a spiritually impoverished life?

10. Some believers may victoriously dance their way to heaven while others go languishing. The great news is that both find their way home to the City. How does Romans 15:1-6 help us to deal with our differences?

HOPEFUL MISJUDGES LITTLE-FAITH

11. Hopeful is a person of intrinsic hope. Even so, he finds Little-faith annoying. He forgets his own stumbles along the way, and prefers to write off this weaker brother. But instead of criticizing the weak, we should pray for them. What are some elements of Paul's prayer in Ephesians 3:16-19 that provide a helpful model as we pray for each other? Also, how does he warn us in 1 Corinthians 10:12?

12. Have you ever met the thieving "three big bruisers" (Faint-heart, Mistrust, and Guilt) in your pilgrimage? From your experience, how would you advise others to find relief from their affliction?

13. (*) Look at Isaiah 42:3, 1 John 2:1-2, and Romans 8:1, 31-39. How might you use these Scriptures to minister to one in Little-faith's paralyzed condition?

14. Why does Christian express empathy for Little-faith? Why do you think this is an important perspective?

15. How does Romans 12:3, 16 advise us to adjust our attitudes? What does Proverbs 18:12 say about this?

~~~~~~~~~~~~~~~~~~~~~~~~~~

~~~~~~~~~~~~~~~~~~~~~~~~~

GREAT-GRACE AND FIGHTING THE GOOD FIGHT

16. Nearly everyone loves a champion, and Great-grace is the King's champion. What does his name tell you about him? The Apostle Paul was a King's champion. What does he say about it in 1 Corinthians 15:10?

17. According to Christian, what two things should we do to prevent being robbed on the King's Highway? What do they mean to you?

    a.

    b.

Key Pilgrim's Perspective

No one wants to be a weak and whining pilgrim. We all prefer to be a valiant champion. The truth is that even the best champions suffer battle wounds and times of weakness. Christian cites David, Heman, Hezekiah, and Peter as examples. The great news is that God gives grace, and grace makes the difference. Rather than striving for greatness, we should humbly learn to rely on God's grace for our salvation, victory, and spiritual growth. Joel 3:10 says, "Let the weak say, 'I am strong.'" When walking in grace, we can say, "I am strong." Always remember that no matter how strong in faith you would become, it will take God's grace. (Applicable Scripture for the champions cited above can be found in 1 Samuel 21:11-13; Psalm 88; 2 Kings 20:1-3; Matthew 26:35, 69-72.)

18. Christian acknowledges that God's grace has brought him through his battles. Does he believe his battles are over? When Paul advised Timothy in 1 Timothy 6:12, "Fight the good fight of faith," do you believe he spoke of a passing skirmish or a lifetime campaign? How do you interpret this for your life?

19. Do you have areas in your life where you'd like to see less Little-faith and more Great-grace? Look at James 4:6-7. How can you apply this Scripture to your own pilgrimage? Write a prayer based on what you want to see in your life.

Scriptures for Further Reflection

Psalm 125:4-5
Proverbs 12:1-6
Luke 13:24-29
Hebrews 10:36-39
2 Thessalonians 2:16-17
1 Corinthians 3:11-13
Isaiah 35:3-4
Luke 17:5-6

NOTES:

SCRIPTURES USED IN THIS CHAPTER

Romans 11:25
Lest you be wise in your own conceits, I want you to understand this mystery, brothers: a partial hardening has come upon Israel, until the fullness of the Gentiles has come in.

Luke 18:9-14
He also told this parable to some who trusted in themselves that they were righteous, and treated others with contempt: [10]"Two men went up into the temple to pray, one a Pharisee and the other a tax collector. [11]The Pharisee, standing by himself, prayed thus: 'God, I thank you that I am not like other men, extortioners, unjust, adulterers, or even like this tax collector.
[12]I fast twice a week; I give tithes of all that I get.' [13]But the tax collector, standing far off, would not even lift up his eyes to heaven, but beat his breast, saying, 'God, be merciful to me, a sinner!' [14]I tell you, this man went down to his house justified, rather than the other. For everyone who exalts himself will be humbled, but the one who humbles himself will be exalted."

Matthew 12:43-45
"When the unclean spirit has gone out of a person, it passes through waterless places seeking rest, but finds none. [44]Then it says, 'I will return to my house from which I came.' And when it comes, it finds the house empty, swept, and put in order. [45]Then it goes and brings with it seven other spirits more evil than itself, and they enter and dwell there, and the last state of that person is worse than the first. So also will it be with this evil generation."

James 1:14-15
But each person is tempted when he is lured and enticed by his own desire. [15]Then desire when it has conceived gives birth to sin, and sin when it is fully grown brings forth death.

Proverbs 4:23, 22:5, 23:19, 28:26 NIV
[4:23]Above all else, guard your heart, for it is the wellspring of life. [22:5]In the paths of the wicked lie thorns and snares, but he who guards his soul stays far from them. [23:19]Listen, my son, and be wise, and keep your heart on the right path. [28:26]He who trusts in himself is a fool, but he who walks in wisdom is kept safe.

Romans 15:1-6
We who are strong have an obligation to bear with the failings of the weak, and not to please ourselves. [2]Let each of us please his neighbor for his good, to build him up. [3]For Christ did not please himself, but as it is written, "The reproaches of those who reproached you fell on me." [4]For whatever was written in former days was written for our instruction, that through endurance and through the encouragement of the Scriptures we might have hope. [5]May the God of endurance and encouragement grant you to live in such harmony with one another, in accord with Christ Jesus, [6]that together you may with one voice glorify the God and Father of our Lord Jesus Christ.

Ephesians 3:16-19 NIV
I pray that out of his glorious riches he may strengthen you with power through his Spirit in your inner being, [17]so that Christ may dwell in your hearts through faith. And I pray that you, being rooted and established in love, [18]may have power, together with all the saints, to grasp how wide and long and high and deep is the love of Christ, [19]and to know this love that surpasses knowledge—that you may be filled to the measure of all the fullness of God.

1 Corinthians 10:12
Therefore let anyone who thinks that he stands take heed lest he fall.

Isaiah 42:3
A bruised reed he will not break, and a faintly burning wick he will not quench; he will faithfully bring forth justice.

1 John 2:1-2 NIV

My dear children, I write this to you so that you will not sin. But if anybody does sin, we have one who speaks to the Father in our defense—Jesus Christ, the Righteous One. [2]He is the atoning sacrifice for our sins, and not only for ours but also for the sins of the whole world.

Romans 8:1, 31-39

[1]There is therefore now no condemnation for those who are in Christ Jesus. What then shall we say to these things? If God is for us, who can be against us? [32]He who did not spare his own Son but gave him up for us all, how will he not also with him graciously give us all things? [33]Who shall bring any charge against God's elect? It is God who justifies. [34]Who is to condemn? Christ Jesus is the one who died—more than that, who was raised—who is at the right hand of God, who indeed is interceding for us. [35]Who shall separate us from the love of Christ? Shall tribulation, or distress, or persecution, or famine, or nakedness, or danger, or sword? [36]As it is written, "For your sake we are being killed all the day long; we are regarded as sheep to be slaughtered." [37]No, in all these things we are more than conquerors through him who loved us. [38]For I am sure that neither death nor life, nor angels nor rulers, nor things present nor things to come, nor powers, [39]nor height nor depth, nor anything else in all creation, will be able to separate us from the love of God in Christ Jesus our Lord.

Romans 12:3, 16

[3]For by the grace given to me I say to everyone among you not to think of himself more highly than he ought to think, but to think with sober judgment, each according to the measure of faith that God has assigned. [16]Live in harmony with one another. Do not be haughty, but associate with the lowly. Never be conceited.

Proverbs 18:12

Before destruction a man's heart is haughty, but humility comes before honor.

1 Corinthians 15:10

But by the grace of God I am what I am, and his grace toward me was not in vain. On the contrary, I worked harder than any of them, though it was not I, but the grace of God that is with me.

1 Timothy 6:12

Fight the good fight of the faith. Take hold of the eternal life to which you were called and about which you made the good confession in the presence of many witnesses.

James 4:6-7

But he gives more grace. Therefore it says, "God opposes the proud, but gives grace to the humble." [7]Submit yourselves therefore to God. Resist the devil, and he will flee from you.

CHAPTER

TO BEGIN

"By now, I should have known better." Have you ever said this to yourself? Explain.

THE PILGRIMS ARE DECEIVED

1. In the last chapter, Christian and Hopeful discuss three violent robbers. Not every danger, however, is bold and confrontational. What confuses the pilgrims as they continue their pilgrimage?

2. This time, the pilgrims don't peer over a wall at forbidden ground; however, trouble still finds them. What does the white-robed man depict to you? Can one dressed in white be as dangerous as one dressed in black? How does 2 Corinthians 11:14-15 apply?

3. Do you think that as we progress in our Christian walk and become wiser, the enemy uses more devious schemes against us? How do Genesis 3:1 and 2 Corinthians 11:3 describe him?

4. In Matthew 24:3-4, the disciples wanted more clarity about the signs preceding Christ's return. But He chose to warn them, instead. What was His warning?

5. Paul told the Church of Galatia that they astonished him (but not in a good way). In Galatians 1:6-9, what charge does he level at them?

6. We do not see in Christian and Hopeful a portrait of "perfect" believers. Theirs is more of an up-and-down experience. How do you relate to this in your own pilgrimage?

ENCOUNTER WITH A SHINING ONE

7. Early in his pilgrimage, Christian met shining ones who bore gifts. What does this one carry?

8. The shining one interrogates the pilgrims. It becomes clear Christian and Hopeful made some errors in judgment. What were they?

9. What do you think of the two pilgrims receiving a whipping and then showing gratitude for it? Read and reflect upon Hebrews 12:5-13 and Revelation 3:19. How do these Scriptures speak to you? Can you think of times the Lord has disciplined you? How did you respond? Can you thank God for His discipline?

MEETING ATHEIST

10. (*) In the End Times, we should guard against the influence of scoffers who take pleasure in mocking both God and His people. How does 2 Peter 3:3 warn us against them? How does Galatians 6:7 issue a warning to them?

11. Atheist says he searched out the Way for twenty years and found nothing. How does Jude 1:17-19 identify the core issues of mockers like Atheist? According to 2 Corinthians 5:7, what else makes the difference between an atheist's quest and that of a true pilgrim?

12. Scoffers are insulting and intimidating. Have you met any? If so, did defending yourself prove helpful? What do you think is the best approach when facing them?

13. After their encounter with Atheist, the pilgrims reaffirmed their belief in the truth. Then Hopeful declared, "Now I rejoice in my hope of seeing the glory of God." God's pilgrims do, indeed, have so much reason for rejoicing. But the Lord rejoices, too. What brings joy to His heart in Luke 10:21-23?

ON THE ENCHANTED GROUND

14. Hopeful wants to sleep on the Enchanted Ground, but Christian corrects him. What does this intoxicating ground represent in the Christian life?

15. Sins that plague pilgrims in their turbulent younger years are often easy to identify. Sins in later years, especially when life is good, are perhaps more subtle. These slowly erode faith and resolve. In our culture, what kinds of "enchanting" temptations do you think can lure seasoned pilgrims to sleep?

16. (*) So often, sluggishness leads to sleepiness.

    a. How does Hebrews 6:11-12 address spiritual sluggishness?

    b. How does Mark 13:33-37 address spiritual sleepiness?

17. Many in today's Church seem to be sleeping—in the words of the late Keith Green, "asleep in the light"—when they could make a difference in this desperate world. What does Paul imply in Ephesians 5:14 about sleeping Christians? What does it demand, and what does it promise?

18. Paul continues his thought in Ephesians 5:15-16. Describe any ways you can apply his admonition to your own pilgrimage.

19. The two pilgrims help each other stay awake and disenchanted with this numbing worldly spirit. How do other believers and you keep each other safe from an encroaching desire for spiritual slumber? Can you think of ways to improve?

~~~~~~~~~~~~~~~~~~~~~~~~~~~~~~~

Scriptures for Further Reflection

Matthew 24:4-5, 11, 23-27
Psalm 140:5
Micah 6:8
Daniel 11:32
Romans 1:18
Proverbs 3:11-12
2 Corinthians 4:3-4

~~~~~~~~~~~~~~~~~~~~~~~~~~~~~~~

NOTES:

SCRIPTURES USED IN THIS CHAPTER

2 Corinthians 11:14-15
And no wonder, for even Satan disguises himself as an angel of light. [15]So it is no surprise if his servants, also, disguise themselves as servants of righteousness. Their end will correspond to their deeds.

Genesis 3:1
Now the serpent was more crafty than any other beast of the field that the LORD God had made. He said to the woman, "Did God actually say, 'You shall not eat of any tree in the garden'?"

2 Corinthians 11:3
But I am afraid that as the serpent deceived Eve by his cunning, your thoughts will be led astray from a sincere and pure devotion to Christ.

Matthew 24:3-4
As he sat on the Mount of Olives, the disciples came to him privately, saying, "Tell us, when will these things be, and what will be the sign of your coming and of the close of the age?" [4]And Jesus answered them, "See that no one leads you astray.

Galatians 1:6-9 NLT
I am shocked that you are turning away so soon from God, who called you to himself through the loving mercy of Christ. You are following a different way that pretends to be the Good News [7]but is not the Good News at all. You are being fooled by those who deliberately twist the truth concerning Christ. [8]Let God's curse fall on anyone, including us or even an angel from heaven, who preaches a different kind of Good News than the one we preached to you. [9]I say again what we have said before: If anyone preaches any other Good News than the one you welcomed, let that person be cursed.

Hebrews 12:5-13 NLT
And have you forgotten the encouraging words God spoke to you as his children? He said, "My child, don't make light of the LORD's discipline, and don't give up when he corrects you. [6]For the LORD disciplines those he loves, and he punishes each one he accepts as his child." [7]As you endure this divine discipline, remember that God is treating you as his own children. Who ever heard of a child who is never disciplined by its father? [8]If God doesn't discipline you as he does all of his children, it means that you are illegitimate and are not really his children at all. [9]Since we respected our earthly fathers who disciplined us, shouldn't we submit even more to the discipline of the Father of our spirits, and live forever? [10]For our earthly fathers disciplined us for a few years, doing the best they knew how. But God's discipline is always good for us, so that we might share in his holiness. [11]No discipline is enjoyable while it is happening — it's painful! But afterward there will be a peaceful harvest of right living for those who are trained in this way. [12]So take a new grip with your tired hands and strengthen your weak knees. [13]Mark out a straight path for your feet so that those who are weak and lame will not fall but become strong.

Revelation 3:19
Those whom I love, I reprove and discipline, so be zealous and repent.

2 Peter 3:3 NLT
Most importantly, I want to remind you that in the last days scoffers will come, mocking the truth and following their own desires.

Galatians 6:7
Do not be deceived: God is not mocked, for whatever one sows, that will he also reap.

Jude 1:17-19

But you must remember, beloved, the predictions of the apostles of our Lord Jesus Christ. [18]They said to you, "In the last time there will be scoffers, following their own ungodly passions." [19]It is these who cause divisions, worldly people, devoid of the Spirit.

2 Corinthians 5:7

For we walk by faith, not by sight.

Luke 10:21-23

In that same hour he rejoiced in the Holy Spirit and said, "I thank you, Father, Lord of heaven and earth, that you have hidden these things from the wise and understanding and revealed them to little children; yes, Father, for such was your gracious will. [22]All things have been handed over to me by my Father, and no one knows who the Son is except the Father, or who the Father is except the Son and anyone to whom the Son chooses to reveal him." [23]Then turning to the disciples he said privately, "Blessed are the eyes that see what you see!

Hebrews 6:11-12

And we desire each one of you to show the same earnestness to have the full assurance of hope until the end, [12]so that you may not be sluggish, but imitators of those who through faith and patience inherit the promises.

Mark 13:33-37

Be on guard, keep awake. For you do not know when the time will come. [34]It is like a man going on a journey, when he leaves home and puts his servants in charge, each with his work, and commands the doorkeeper to stay awake. [35]Therefore stay awake—for you do not know when the master of the house will come, in the evening, or at midnight, or when the cock crows, or in the morning— [36]lest he come suddenly and find you asleep. [37]And what I say to you I say to all: Stay awake.

Ephesians 5:14b

Therefore it says, "Awake, O sleeper, and arise from the dead, and Christ will shine on you."

Ephesians 5:15-16

Look carefully then how you walk, not as unwise but as wise, [16]making the best use of the time, because the days are evil.

CHAPTER

~~~~~~~~~~~~~~~~~~~~~~~~

Progress Memory Verse

For there is only one God and one Mediator who can reconcile God and humanity — the man Christ Jesus. He gave his life to purchase freedom for everyone. This is the message God gave to the world at just the right time.

--1 Timothy 2:5-6

~~~~~~~~~~~~~~~~~~~~~~~~

TO BEGIN

Is the story of your conversion to Christ worth sharing? Of course, it is. Have you shared it? With whom? How can you make better use of your wonderful story?

HOPEFUL TELLS HIS STORY

1. This chapter opens with Christian asking Hopeful about his pilgrimage and Hopeful replying with a short definition of his pilgrimage. What does this mean to you?

2. The pilgrims shake off the Enchanted Ground's bewitching spell by talking about their personal experiences. Have you found that sharing your testimony and beliefs, as well as listening to those of others, help enliven you spiritually? Why?

3. Prior to his conversion, Hopeful lived in Vanity Fair. He says that while living there, he delighted "in those things that are seen, which were sold at our fair." Read 2 Corinthians 4:17-18 and Hebrews 11:1. What do the seen and unseen represent?

4. (*) Hopeful recalls the things he once enjoyed at the fair. Reflecting on how far God has brought us since coming to Christ can renew our devotion. Evaluate your former life through the eyes of faith. What kind of things did you lack that you now possess?

~~~~~~

Progress Quotes from Other Pilgrims

And now let me address all of you, high and low, rich and poor, one with another, to accept of mercy and grace while it is offered to you; Now is the accepted time, now is the day of salvation; and will you not accept it, now it is offered to you?

--George Whitfield

The Gospel is good news of mercy to the undeserving. The symbol of the religion of Jesus is the cross, not the scales.

--John Stott

~~~~~~

5. Hopeful says that Christian and Faithful's words about death, wrath, and disobedience set in motion a struggle in him over sin and damnation. Our current culture largely views God's truth as too narrow, extreme, and insulting. Do you think this influences believers to be too cautious about using convicting words of truth? What do you think we should do?

6. (*) At first, it would appear that Christian and Faithful's witness in Vanity Fair was fruitless. Yet, Hopeful came along later. Perhaps we should concern ourselves less with results and more with faithfulness to our calling. What things can we learn from Paul's approach to evangelism in Ephesians 6:19-20 and Acts 20:20-21, 24?

7. Hopeful's conversion took some time. What were the four reasons he gave for resisting the Holy Spirit's conviction?

8. (*) Conviction of sin hounded Hopeful. In John 16:8, what does Jesus say of the Holy Spirit's ministry?

ATTEMPTED REFORMS AND RENEWED CONVICTION

9. When Hopeful feared going to Hell, how did he try to alleviate his guilt?

10. Scriptures plagued Hopeful, including Isaiah 64:6. According to this, why would all of our best efforts be doomed to failure?

11. Christianity is the one belief-system that does not offer a works-based way of salvation; yet even in the Church multitudes misunderstand this. Look again at Ephesians 2:8-10. What does it say about salvation and works?

~~~~~~

Key Pilgrim's Perspective

Hopeful described the dilemma of owing an impossible debt to God. Even if he somehow reformed his present life, he could never get out from under the accumulated debt of his past one.

In the temporal world, people file bankruptcy so they can have their debts discharged and escape personal liability. Spiritually, however, the situation is far worse. In ourselves, we can do nothing to discharge our enormous debt before God. In His courtroom, He is both judge and creditor. Standing before Him as guilty and insolvent sinners, we have nothing of merit to offer. Even our best efforts are futile against the eternal prison of Hell we deserve.

Praise God for Jesus! He paid the price for our debt of sin, so we are set free! In the words of Ellis J. Crum, "He paid a debt He did not owe; I owed a debt I could not pay; I needed someone to wash my sins away." Receiving the eternal "debt relief" that Jesus offers is as simple as humbling ourselves, admitting our plight, repenting of our sins, and accepting His forgiveness. His grace covers it all.

~~~~~~

THE DEBT AND POWER OF SIN

12. Hopeful describes two difficulties that thwart his efforts to stand guiltless before God. What are they?

13. Are you convinced of your complete helplessness to please God by your own efforts? Describe when the light went on that caused you to lean your full weight on God's grace.

A SAVIOR IS NEEDED

14. Hopeful came and poured out his heart to Faithful. Based on Colossians 4:5-6, why might Hopeful have wanted to come to Faithful? Can you see unbelievers turning to you in their hour of decision? How might you make this more a reality in your life?

~~~~~~~~~~~~~~~~~~~~~~~~

Progress Tip

Faithful was martyred in Vanity Fair. Hopeful witnessed this brutal treatment and yet came to realize that he was the one who was truly dead. What looked like a defeat for the Gospel actually sparked great interest in the Gospel. Be prepared to share your Christian testimony and relevant Scriptures. The Holy Spirit earnestly seeks those whom He can use to help lost souls to salvation in Christ.

~~~~~~~~~~~~~~~~~~~~~~~~

15. Most all religions, cults, and -isms try to include a place for Jesus Christ. To them, He is one in a plethora of religious leaders, prophets, etc. Faithful, however, described Him to Hopeful in a way that sets Him apart from everyone else. What did he say?

16. When Hopeful expressed objections to faith in Christ, to whom did Faithful direct him? How is this approach like that of Philip with Nathaniel? (See John 1:45-46.)

17. Faithful directed Hopeful to a second place for answers. What is it? According to 2 Timothy 3:15, why is this a good idea?

18. To unrepentant sinners, Christ's throne will be a seat of judgment. When Faithful directed Hopeful to the throne, what did he call it? How does Jesus portray His throne in Matthew 25:31-33, 46?

~~~~~~~~~~~~~~~~~~~~~~~~~~~

Definition: Mercy Seat

Under the Old Covenant, the mercy seat was a slab of pure gold. It sat over the Ark of the Covenant and represented God's throne. Once a year, on the Day of Atonement, the High Priest would sprinkle it with animal blood. This absolved the people of their sins and reconciled them to God.

Jesus Christ is the High Priest and Mediator of the New Covenant. Symbolically, He sits on the mercy seat that is sprinkled in His blood. Now, because of that sprinkling, those who trust in Him no longer face a throne of judgment. God is merciful only through Christ. Outside of Christ, there is no mercy.

~~~~~~~~~~~~~~~~~~~~~~~~~~~

19. Faithful described a good "sinner's prayer" for Hopeful. What significant elements of this prayer would be useful to remember when leading someone in a prayer to receive Christ?

HE RECEIVES A REVELATION

20. At last, many Scriptures came together for Hopeful. What did he finally understand that gave him joy?

21. Besides growing in joy, Hopeful experienced what other changes in his life?

22. Hopeful describes the great love he felt for Christ as a new believer. Older and more mature now, he still might have succumbed to the Enchanted Ground's dulling spirit. But Christian prodded him to stay awake by reflecting on his Christian testimony. This revived his spirit. How do Luke 21:36 and Hebrews 10:24-25 speak to our responsibility both for our own spiritual condition and for that of other believers?

23. In this chapter, the pilgrims spent time reflecting on Christ's greatness and goodness. Take a few moments to do that, too. Write a prayer of praise and gratitude for all He means to you.

~~~~~~~~~~~~~~~~~~~~~~~~

Scriptures for Further Reflection

Acts 3:19; 17:30-31
Romans 3:23
2 Corinthians 7:10
Psalm 38:3-6
Job 15:14-16
John 6:63
Colossians 1:21-22
2 Corinthians 2:15-16

~~~~~~~~~~~~~~~~~~~~~~~~

NOTES:

_____

_____

_____

_____

_____

_____

_____

_____

_____

_____

_____

_____

_____

_____

_____

_____

_____

_____

_____

_____

_____

_____

SCRIPTURES USED IN THIS CHAPTER

2 Corinthians 4:17-18

For this slight momentary affliction is preparing for us an eternal weight of glory beyond all comparison, [18]as we look not to the things that are seen but to the things that are unseen. For the things that are seen are transient, but the things that are unseen are eternal.

Hebrews 11:1 NIV

Now faith is being sure of what we hope for and certain of what we do not see.

Ephesians 6:19-20 NLT

And pray for me, too. Ask God to give me the right words so I can boldly explain God's mysterious plan that the Good News is for Jews and Gentiles alike. [20]I am in chains now, still preaching this message as God's ambassador. So pray that I will keep on speaking boldly for him, as I should.

Acts 20:20-21, 24 NLT

I never shrank back from telling you what you needed to hear, either publicly or in your homes. [21]I have had one message for Jews and Greeks alike — the necessity of repenting from sin and turning to God, and of having faith in our Lord Jesus. [24]But my life is worth nothing to me unless I use it for finishing the work assigned me by the Lord Jesus — the work of telling others the Good News about the wonderful grace of God.

John 16:8 NLT

And when he comes, he will convict the world of its sin, and of God's righteousness, and of the coming judgment.

Isaiah 64:6 NLT

We are all infected and impure with sin. When we display our righteous deeds, they are nothing but filthy rags. Like autumn leaves, we wither and fall, and our sins sweep us away like the wind.

Ephesians 2:8-10

For by grace you have been saved through faith. And this is not your own doing; it is the gift of God, [9]not a result of works, so that no one may boast. [10]For we are his workmanship, created in Christ Jesus for good works, which God prepared beforehand, that we should walk in them.

Colossians 4:5-6

Conduct yourselves wisely toward outsiders, making the best use of the time. 6 Let your speech always be gracious, seasoned with salt, so that you may know how you ought to answer each person.

John 1:45-46

Philip found Nathanael and said to him, "We have found him of whom Moses in the Law and also the prophets wrote, Jesus of Nazareth, the son of Joseph." [46]Nathanael said to him, "Can anything good come out of Nazareth?" Philip said to him, "Come and see."

2 Timothy 3:15 NLT

You have been taught the holy Scriptures from childhood, and they have given you the wisdom to receive the salvation that comes by trusting in Christ Jesus.

Matthew 25:31-33, 46

"When the Son of Man comes in his glory, and all the angels with him, then he will sit on his glorious throne. [32]Before him will be gathered all the nations, and he will separate people one from another as a shepherd separates the sheep from the goats. [33]And he will place the sheep on his right, but the goats on the left. [46]And these will go away into eternal punishment, but the righteous into eternal life."

Luke 21:36

But stay awake at all times, praying that you may have strength to escape all these things that are going to take place, and to stand before the Son of Man.

Hebrews 10:24

And let us consider how to stir up one another to love and good works. . .

CHAPTER

16

~~~~~~~~~~~~~~~~~~~~~~~~

Progress Memory Verse

Fear of the LORD is the foundation of wisdom. Knowledge of the Holy One results in good judgment.

--Proverbs 9:10 NLT

~~~~~~~~~~~~~~~~~~~~~~~~

TO BEGIN

Have you been in a mentoring relationship with someone? Can you recall a memorable moment in this relationship?

THE PILGRIMS DISCUSS JUSTIFICATION WITH IGNORANCE

1. Christian and Hopeful are older and wiser pilgrims. But that doesn't seem to matter to Ignorance. Why does he prefer to hang back from them?

2. Our "tolerant" culture would think it unjustified and impolite to correct Ignorance's beliefs. Should the pilgrims simply let the man live out the truth as he sees it? What is the reason for your thinking?

~~~~~~~~~~~~~~~~~~~~~~~

Note:

Remember that Ignorance never joined the Way by coming through the Wicket Gate. Instead, he entered by way of a crooked lane leading from his own country of Conceit. Taking such a path, he avoided the Cross and other places such as the Valley of Humiliation.

~~~~~~~~~~~~~~~~~~~~~~~

3. Christian and Hopeful have a relationship that includes accountability. Ignorance does not. Look at Ecclesiastes 4:9-10, James 5:16, and Galatians 6:1. How do these verses speak to this issue of accountability?

4. Ignorance wants salvation but only on his terms. How do his aspiration and positive thinking contrast with the spiritual condition Paul describes in Romans 7:18-25?

5. What does Jesus say in Luke 14:33 that it takes to be His disciple? What does Peter claim in Matthew 19:27? Ignorance makes the same claim as Peter, but does he have that right? In your opinion, what kind of things has he yet to surrender?

6. Ignorance believes his heart is good because his heart tells him so. What does Jeremiah 17:9-10 have to say about this?

7. According to Christian, what is the nature of truly good thoughts about ourselves? How does Ignorance respond to this?

8. (*) God's Word in some ways can be like a spiritual sobriety test to tell us whether or not we are truly walking a straight line. How do 2 Timothy 3:16-17 and James 1:25 speak to this? Do you see areas of personal intoxication where you can use God's intervention? Pray about this.

9. To Ignorance, a proper view of God (good thoughts) is defined by his own subjective concepts. To Christian, such beliefs must align themselves with the objective truth of God's Word. Christian cites some "good thoughts" related to God and how He views humanity. What are they?

~~~~~~

Key Pilgrim's Perspective

We may be able to fool ourselves, and we can fool others. God, however, sees the true condition of our hearts; we can never fool Him. Ignorance well illustrates today's culture. Consciences of many are seared, affections perverted, and souls darkened. Yet, so many see themselves as enlightened. God says, "Woe to those who call evil good, and good evil; who put darkness for light, and light for darkness; who put bitter for sweet, and sweet for bitter! Woe to those who are wise in their own eyes, and prudent in their own sight!" (Isaiah 5:20-21). Today, persuasive voices call from many directions. Good pilgrims learn to heed God's Word and listen to the still, small voice of His Spirit.

~~~~~~

10. Ignorance says he trusts Christ for his justification before God. But he doesn't really. How does he, in actuality, trust in his own good works?

11. (*) Chew a bit on Romans 3:10-12, 20-28; 5:1-2. How do these verses speak to your own salvation experience?

12. Christian identifies three characteristics of Ignorance's confession of faith. In a nutshell, what are they, and what reason does Christian give for each view? What consequence does Christian see for this belief?

    a.

    b.

    c.

    d. Consequence:

13. Christian counters Ignorance's false confession of faith with the true one. How does he define true justifying faith?

14. Ignorance voices the age-old argument that faith in Christ alone for salvation opens people to sinful indulgence. Christian contends that the true effect of saving faith is reverence for Christ in our lives. Consider your own heart and life. What motivates you more: love and reverence for Christ, or some kind of striving for worthiness and acceptance? Be sure to pray over any confusion you feel about this.

15. (*) Revelations by God's Spirit seem irrational and unfounded to those like Ignorance their religious spirits. Let's look at three related Scriptures:

    Matthew 11:25-26: What made Jesus thankful here?

    Ephesians 1:15-21: What did Paul pray God would give us for enabling us to see His many Kingdom riches?

    Proverbs 29:18: What does this say about revelation?

    What is a meaningful revelation you have received?

~~~~~~~~~~~~~~~~~~~~~~~~~~

Progress Quote from Another Pilgrim

Either sin is with you, lying on your shoulders, or it is lying on Christ, the Lamb of God. Now if it is lying on your back, you are lost; but if it is resting on Christ, you are free, and you will be saved. Now choose what you want.

-- Martin Luther

~~~~~~~~~~~~~~~~~~~~~~~~~~

16. Christian implores Ignorance to awaken to his lost condition. Rejecting the entreaty, Ignorance chooses to continue in his deception. Does the Bible address the issue of self-deception? (See 1 Corinthians 3:18; Galatians. 6:3; and James 1:22.) Ask the Lord to reveal any areas of self-deception in your life. Pray about this.

THEY DISCUSS GODLY FEAR

17. The pilgrims discuss godly fear. Ignorance fears exposure more than he fears the Lord. Rather than admit guilt, he suppresses any conviction of sin. In the previous question, we looked at self-deception.

Do you still need to come clean with God in some area? Let Him take it now. Record anything memorable you feel He's impressing upon you.

~~~~~~

Definition: Godly Fear

The Bible mentions fear as the usual response to God. Godly fear has two senses – danger and reverence. Fear of danger comes as people see their sin and anticipate Divine punishment (e.g. Genesis 3:10; 20:8). The fullest expression is seen in End-time events (e.g. Revelation 6:15-16). Godly fear also results from a revelation of the Lord's overwhelming glory (e.g. Exodus 20:18-20; Luke 2:9-10). This reverential fear evokes deep feelings of awe and wonder, and becomes a believer's primary motivation. Not cowering or slavish, it is the respectful fear of beloved children toward their Father. No longer fearing wrath, they trust their Father's grace and love. Godly fear leads believers to worship God and live faithful lives in obedience to His precepts.

~~~~~~

18. According to Christian, what is so wonderful about godly fear?

19. (*) Christian cites reasons people try to stifle godly fear. Hopeful admits he was like this before understanding these things. We have already seen how Faithful's witness influenced Hopeful. Do you find this encouraging as you consider sharing your faith with those who may, at first, resist? How does Romans 10:13-15 apply to our calling as Christians?

THEY DISCUSS BACKSLIDING

20. The pilgrims discuss Mr. Temporary–living with Mr. Turn-back--who was influenced away from a pilgrimage by one called Save-self. What kind of tendency does Save-self represent?

21. The pilgrims now consider four causes of backsliding. What are they?

   a.

   b.

c.

d.

22. The pilgrims also talk about the progression of backsliding. What are those steps?

a.

b.

c.

d.

e.

f.

g.

h.

23. From the previous question, we see that backsliding doesn't happen all at once but happens by degrees. Evaluate your own heart. Do you see any areas of vulnerability in your own life?

~~~~~~~~~~~~~~~~~~~~~~~~

Scriptures for Further Reflection

1 John 4:6
Philippians 3:8-9
Titus 3:4-7
Romans 8:6-8
Matthew 13:15-16
Romans 4:3-5
2 Corinthians 5:14-15
Revelation 14:6-7

~~~~~~~~~~~~~~~~~~~~~~~~

NOTES:

SCRIPTURES USED IN THIS CHAPTER

Ecclesiastes 4:9-10

Two are better than one, because they have a good reward for their toil. [10]For if they fall, one will lift up his fellow. But woe to him who is alone when he falls and has not another to lift him up!

James 5:16

Therefore, confess your sins to one another and pray for one another, that you may be healed. The prayer of a righteous person has great power as it is working.

Galatians 6:1 NLT

Dear brothers and sisters, if another believer is overcome by some sin, you who are godly should gently and humbly help that person back onto the right path. And be careful not to fall into the same temptation yourself.

Romans 7:18-25

For I know that nothing good dwells in me, that is, in my flesh. For I have the desire to do what is right, but not the ability to carry it out. [19]For I do not do the good I want, but the evil I do not want is what I keep on doing. [20]Now if I do what I do not want, it is no longer I who do it, but sin that dwells within me. [21]So I find it to be a law that when I want to do right, evil lies close at hand. [22]For I delight in the law of God, in my inner being, [23]but I see in my members another law waging war against the law of my mind and making me captive to the law of sin that dwells in my members. [24]Wretched man that I am! Who will deliver me from this body of death? [25]Thanks be to God through Jesus Christ our Lord! So then, I myself serve the law of God with my mind, but with my flesh I serve the law of sin.

Luke 14:33

So therefore, any one of you who does not renounce all that he has cannot be my disciple.

Matthew 19:27

Then Peter said in reply, "See, we have left everything and followed you. What then will we have?"

Jeremiah 17:9-10

The heart is deceitful above all things, and desperately sick; who can understand it? [10]"I the LORD search the heart and test the mind, to give every man according to his ways, according to the fruit of his deeds."

2 Timothy 3:16-17 NLT

All Scripture is inspired by God and is useful to teach us what is true and to make us realize what is wrong in our lives. It corrects us when we are wrong and teaches us to do what is right. [17]God uses it to prepare and equip his people to do every good work.

James 1:25

But the one who looks into the perfect law, the law of liberty, and perseveres, being no hearer who forgets but a doer who acts, he will be blessed in his doing.

Romans 3:10-12, 20-28; 5:1-2 (NLT)

As the Scriptures say, "No one is righteous — not even one. [11]No one is truly wise; no one is seeking God. [12]All have turned away; all have become useless. No one does good, not a single one" . . . . [20]For no one can ever be made right with God by doing what the law commands. The law simply shows us how sinful we are. [21]But now God has shown us a way to be made right with him without keeping the requirements of the law, as was promised in the writings of Moses and the prophets long ago. [22]We are made right with God by placing our faith in Jesus Christ. And this is true for everyone who believes, no matter who we are. [23]For everyone has sinned; we all fall short of God's glorious standard. [24]Yet God, with undeserved kindness, declares that we are righteous. He did this through Christ Jesus when he freed us from the penalty for our sins. [25]For God presented Jesus as the sacrifice for sin. People are made right with God when they believe that Jesus sacrificed his life, shedding his blood. This sacrifice shows that God was being fair when he held back and did not punish those who sinned in times past, [26]for he was looking ahead and including them in what he would do in this present time. God did this to demonstrate his righteousness, for he himself is fair and just, and he declares sinners to be right in his sight when they believe in Jesus. [27]Can we boast, then, that we have done anything to be accepted by God? No, because our acquittal is not based on obeying the law. It is based on faith. [28]So we are made right with God through faith and not by obeying the law. . . . [5:1]Therefore being justified by faith, we have peace with God through our Lord Jesus Christ: [2]By whom also we have access by faith into this grace wherein we stand, and rejoice in hope of the glory of God.

Matthew 11:25-26
At that time Jesus declared, "I thank you, Father, Lord of heaven and earth, that you have hidden these things from the wise and understanding and revealed them to little children; [26]yes, Father, for such was your gracious will."

Ephesians 1:15-21
For this reason, because I have heard of your faith in the Lord Jesus and your love toward all the saints, [16]I do not cease to give thanks for you, remembering you in my prayers, [17]that the God of our Lord Jesus Christ, the Father of glory, may give you a spirit of wisdom and of revelation in the knowledge of him, [18]having the eyes of your hearts enlightened, that you may know what is the hope to which he has called you, what are the riches of his glorious inheritance in the saints, [19]and what is the immeasurable greatness of his power toward us who believe, according to the working of his great might [20]that he worked in Christ when he raised him from the dead and seated him at his right hand in the heavenly places, [21]far above all rule and authority and power and dominion, and above every name that is named, not only in this age but also in the one to come.

Proverbs 29:18 (NIV)
Where there is no revelation, the people cast off restraint; but blessed is he who keeps the law.

1 Corinthians 3:18
Let no one deceive himself. If anyone among you thinks that he is wise in this age, let him become a fool that he may become wise.

Galatians 6:3
For if anyone thinks he is something, when he is nothing, he deceives himself.

James 1:22
But be doers of the word, and not hearers only, deceiving yourselves.

Romans 10:13-15
For "everyone who calls on the name of the Lord will be saved." [14]But how are they to call on him in whom they have not believed? And how are they to believe in him of whom they have never heard? And how are they to hear without someone preaching? [15]And how are they to preach unless they are sent? As it is written, "How beautiful are the feet of those who preach the good news!"

James 5:19-20 NLT
My dear brothers and sisters, if someone among you wanders away from the truth and is brought back, [20]you can be sure that whoever brings the sinner back will save that person from death and bring about the forgiveness of many sins.

CHAPTER

17

TO BEGIN

Name a few things that most delight your heart when you think of heaven.

ENJOYING THE COUNTRY OF BEULAH

1. Christians have long associated Beulah ("married") with the Christian life. Why? (See "Definition: Beulah" (below) and Ephesians 5:25-27, Revelation 19:7-9; 21:9.)

~~~~~~

Definition: Beulah

Isaiah 62:4 says, *You shall no longer be termed Forsaken, Nor shall your land any more be termed Desolate; But you shall be called Hephzibah, and your land Beulah; For the LORD delights in you, And your land shall be married.* (NKJV)

We get the word Beulah in this verse from the Hebrew word, ba'al (baw-al'), which is translated "married."

After Israel broke covenant with God, He sent her into exile. Metaphorically, He called her Forsaken and her land Desolate. But Isaiah prophesied a day of restoration when the land would be renamed Beulah or "Married." This represents the truth that God loves, forgives, and reclaims His people from their brokenness.

Christians adopted Beulah as a popular symbol of the union between Christ and His Church. Beulah was once a common female name. A popular hymn was also entitled, "Beulah Land."

~~~~~~

2. In our story, Beulah is a blessed place that well-tested believers enjoy; a place of confident assurance in our bond with Christ. As you look at your own pilgrimage, where do you see yourself in relation to Beulah?

3. We began in Chapter 1 with Psalm 84:5 as our memory verse. Now look at Psalm 84:7 in relation to coming to the close of the pilgrimage. What can we see about the strength required for undertaking such a journey from beginning to end?

4. In this land where "the covenant between the Bride and the Bridegroom was renewed," we see God portrayed as joyful. Remember that within the covenant relationship of Bride and Groom, there is mutual joy. Do you have trouble seeing God as joyful and even rejoicing over you? What do you think of Scriptures like Isaiah 62:4-5, Zephaniah 3:17, and Nehemiah 8:10?

5. In Beulah, God's promises no longer get whispered to our hearts. What kind of voices did the pilgrims hear coming from the City?

6. The pilgrims aren't yet in the City, but the City is bursting into their souls. They no longer struggle with faint glimpses of eternity. What do they see, and how does that make them feel?

7. (*) Paul had ecstatic heavenly visions that made him long for heaven. What made him feel he needed to stay here longer? What do you think of his example? (See 2 Corinthians 12:1-4 and Philippians 1:21-26.)

8. Bunyan describes the pilgrims' experiences in Beulah in relation to the intense love relationship described in the Song of Solomon. How do these descriptions make you feel about your Lord's love for you? (See Song of Solomon 2:10-13; 7:10-12.)

TWO SHINING ONES

9. In their final hours on earth, the pilgrims prepare for their departure to the City. In these moments, they reminisce with the Shining Ones about the places they have been, and the joys and difficulties they have experienced. When you near the end of your pilgrimage, are there particular memories you will enjoy describing to others?

THE UNAVOIDABLE RIVER

10. Two more difficulties! Describe the first difficulty, which stretches before the two pilgrims and takes them aback.

11. What is this River? Why would the foretastes of heavenly glory suddenly fade at the sight of it?

12. What was Paul's testimony and encouragement to Timothy as he faced his own time of departure? (See 2 Timothy 4:6-8.)

13. (*) Oh, how the pilgrims wish there were another way to the Gate, but there is not. The Shining Ones inform them that only two men have ever avoided this River. Who were they, and how did they avoid it? (See Genesis 5:24 and 2 Kings 2:11.)

14. In the future, those who hear the last trumpet will also escape crossing this River. How? (See 1 Corinthians 15:51-52, 1 Thessalonians 4:16-17.)

15. Death had seemed so desirable to the pilgrims . . . until now. Their bodies are dying, and there is no way to escape but to go through this ordeal. If only they had assurance that it would be easy. Why isn't the River the same depth in every place?

PASSING THROUGH THE RIVER

16. Christian is terrified. Shouldn't he have complete confidence by now? After all, what does 1 John 4:18 say? Why do you think Bunyan chose to depict our hero passing out of this world in such a dark and panic-stricken state?

17. What a great friend Hopeful -- so full of hope – has proved to be. Christian's terror gives way to hope. What does Scripture promise us about hope? (See Romans 5:5.)

ON THE OTHER SIDE

18. The second difficulty the pilgrims face is ascending the mighty Hill to the City. But it turns out to be easy. Why?

WHAT THE PILGRIMS CAN EXPECT AHEAD

19. The Shining Ones give the two pilgrims an orientation before their arrival at the City. What are some of the notable things in their description?

Key Pilgrim's Perspective

On the day we gave our heart to Christ, it was like the day of our betrothal. Christ proposed to us, and we accepted. As wonderful as that day is, the wedding day will be far better. The day He comes for us – either by our dying here or by His second coming –will be our wedding day. We, His spectacularly prepared bride, will be ushered as royalty into heaven's grand wedding hall. Then, we will exult in our Bridegroom's love, and delight together in the Marriage Supper of the Lamb.

Today, we see as through a veil. We do our best, as Heb. 12:2 urges, to fix our eyes on Jesus. Still, we see only in part. One day soon, however, Jesus will lift our wedding veil, and suddenly we will see Him face to face. What an amazing sight that will be! With the eyes of our heart fixed on this awe-inspiring certainty, we can maintain an ardently burning flame in our souls until that glorious day.

20. What will be required of the pilgrims once they enter the City? Name the ones you like best.

A GLAD PROCESSION TO THE GATE

21. (*) What most inspires you about the pilgrims' joyful procession to the gate?

THEY GAIN ENTRANCE TO THE CITY

22. The Shining Ones lead the pilgrims all the way to the City Gate and introduce them. They then present their certificates. This is the "scroll" we saw a Shining One present to Christian at the Cross. What would this indicate?

23. After Christian and Hopeful finally go inside the gate, the scene is glorious. What is the last thing we hear from them?

Progress Tip

Christian and Hopeful finally reach their destination. They can no longer be called "pilgrims and strangers." Their pilgrimages complete, they are Home. This is no fairytale ending; this is the truth plainly expressed in God's Word. In view of this reality, let us decide to conduct our pilgrimage faithfully. Relying upon God's grace and strength, let us never look backward in regret but forward in hope. The end is near. Keeping our eyes fixed on the prize, let us finish strong. Shortly, we will hear those eternally glorious words, "Well done, good and faithful servant. You have been faithful over a few things, I will set you over many things. Enter into the joy of your Lord" (Matthew 25:21, 23).

~~~~~~~~~~~~~~~~~~~~~~~~~~

FINAL OUTCOME OF IGNORANCE

24. Bunyan describes a scene of glory, radiance, and ecstatic bliss. Yet, he does not end his story with this exuberant scene. Where does he end it? Describe the backstory that led to this horrid outcome.

25. Why do you think Bunyan chose to end his story with a tragic scene? Would you have ended this story differently? Why?

IN CLOSING

26. Read Pastor Edward Payson's Letter to His Sister below. Record any thoughts and inspiration you receive from this reading:

Pastor Edward Payson's Letter to His Sister

Edward Payson, D.D. was born July 25, 1783. He was pastor of The Second Church in Portland, Maine. At the age of 43, he became ill and suffered terribly for the next year. On October 22, 1827, he passed into the Celestial City. Shortly before he left this earth, however, he gathered his strength and dictated the following letter to his sister:

My Dear Sister,

Were I to adopt the figurative language of Bunyan, I might date this letter from the land of Beulah, of which I have been for some weeks a happy inhabitant. The celestial city is full in my view. Its glories beam upon me, its breezes fan me, its odors are wafted to me, its sounds strike upon my ears, and its spirit is breathed into my heart. Nothing separates me from it but the river of death, which now appears but as an insignificant rill that may be crossed at a single step, whenever God shall give permission. The Sun of Righteousness has been gradually drawing nearer and nearer, appearing larger and brighter as He approached, and now He fills the whole hemisphere; pouring forth a flood of glory in which I seem to float like an insect in the beams of the sun; exulting, yet almost trembling, while I gaze on this excessive brightness, and wondering, with unutterable wonder, why God should deign thus to shine upon a sinful worm. A single heart and a single tongue seem altogether inadequate to my wants: I want a whole heart for every separate emotion, and a whole tongue to express that emotion.

But why do I speak thus of myself and my feelings? Why not speak only of our God and Redeemer? It is because I know not what to say. When I would speak of them, my words are all swallowed up. I can only tell you what effects their presence produces, and even of these I can tell you but very little. Oh, my sister, my sister! Could you but know what awaits the Christian; could you only, know so much as I know, you could not refrain from rejoicing, and even leaping for joy. Labors, trials, troubles would be nothing: you would rejoice in afflictions, and glory in tribulations; and, like Paul and Silas, sing God's praises in the darkest night, and in the deepest dungeon. You have known a little of my trials and conflicts, and know that they have been neither few nor small; and I hope this glorious termination of them will serve to strengthen your faith, and elevate your hope.

And now, my dear, DEAR sister, farewell. Hold on your Christian course but a few days longer, and you will meet, in heaven,

Your happy and affectionate brother,

Edward Payson

(Public domain)

~~~~~~~~~~~~~~~~~~~~~~~~~~~~

Scriptures for Further Reflection

Isaiah 54:4-8
Lamentations 3:54-57
2 Timothy 1:10
2 Corinthians 5:1-4
1 Corinthians 15:53-55.
Revelation 14:13
1 Corinthians 6:2-3
Psalm 116:15
Hebrews 9:27

~~~~~~~~~~~~~~~~~~~~~~~~~~~~

~~~~~~~~~~~~~~~~~~~~~~~~~~~~

O how blessed to be a pilgrim,
Guided by the Father's hand;
Free at last from every burden
We shall enter Canaan's land.

Songs of victory there shall greet us,
Like the thundering of a mighty flood,
Endless praises be to Jesus,
Who redeemed us by his blood!

O may none give up the journey,
Left in darkness on the shore,
May we all at last be gathered
When our pilgrimage is over.

-- Robert Lowry (Public Domain)

~~~~~~~~~~~~~~~~~~~~~~~~~~~~

NOTES:

SCRIPTURES USED IN THIS CHAPTER

Ephesians 5:25-27

Husbands, love your wives, as Christ loved the church and gave himself up for her, [26]that he might sanctify her, having cleansed her by the washing of water with the word, [27]so that he might present the church to himself in splendor, without spot or wrinkle or any such thing, that she might be holy and without blemish.

Revelation 19:7-9; 21:9

[19:7-9]Let us rejoice and exult and give him the glory, for the marriage of the Lamb has come, and his Bride has made herself ready; [8]it was granted her to clothe herself with fine linen, bright and pure"— for the fine linen is the righteous deeds of the saints. [9]And the angel said to me, "Write this: Blessed are those who are invited to the marriage supper of the Lamb." And he said to me, "These are the true words of God." [21:9]Then came one of the seven angels who had the seven bowls full of the seven last plagues and spoke to me, saying, "Come, I will show you the Bride, the wife of the Lamb."

Psalm 84:5, 7 (WEB)

[5]Blessed are those whose strength is in you; who have set their hearts on a pilgrimage. [7]They go from strength to strength. Everyone of them appears before God in Zion.

Isaiah 62:4-5

You shall no more be termed Forsaken, and your land shall no more be termed Desolate, but you shall be called My Delight Is in Her, and your land Married; for the LORD delights in you, and your land shall be married. [5]For as a young man marries a young woman, so shall your sons marry you, and as the bridegroom rejoices over the bride, so shall your God rejoice over you.

Zephaniah 3:17

The LORD your God is in your midst, a mighty one who will save; he will rejoice over you with gladness; he will quiet you by his love; he will exult over you with loud singing.

Nehemiah 8:10 NLT

And Nehemiah continued, "Go and celebrate with a feast of rich foods and sweet drinks, and share gifts of food with people who have nothing prepared. This is a sacred day before our Lord. Don't be dejected and sad, for the joy of the LORD is your strength!"

2 Corinthians 12:1-4

I must go on boasting. Though there is nothing to be gained by it, I will go on to visions and revelations of the Lord. [2]I know a man in Christ who fourteen years ago was caught up to the third heaven—whether in the body or out of the body I do not know, God knows. [3]And I know that this man was caught up into paradise—whether in the body or out of the body I do not know, God knows— [4]and he heard things that cannot be told, which man may not utter.

Philippians 1:21-26 NLT

For to me, living means living for Christ, and dying is even better. [22]But if I live, I can do more fruitful work for Christ. So I really don't know which is better. [23]I'm torn between two desires: I long to go and be with Christ, which would be far better for me. [24]But for your sakes, it is better that I continue to live. [25]Knowing this, I am convinced that I will remain alive so I can continue to help all of you grow and experience the joy of your faith. [26]And when I come to you again, you will have even more reason to take pride in Christ Jesus because of what he is doing through me.

Song of Solomon 2:10-13; 7:10-12

My beloved speaks and says to me: "Arise, my love, my beautiful one, and come away, [11]for behold, the winter is past; the rain is over and gone. [12]The flowers appear on the earth, the time of singing has come, and the voice of the turtledove is heard in our land. [13]The fig tree ripens its figs, and the vines are in blossom; they give forth fragrance.

Arise, my love, my beautiful one, and come away. 7:10-12I am my beloved's, and his desire is for me. 11Come, my beloved, let us go out into the fields and lodge in the villages; 12let us go out early to the vineyards and see whether the vines have budded, whether the grape blossoms have opened and the pomegranates are in bloom. There I will give you my love.

2 Timothy 4:6-8 NLT

As for me, my life has already been poured out as an offering to God. The time of my death is near. 7I have fought the good fight, I have finished the race, and I have remained faithful. 8And now the prize awaits me — the crown of righteousness, which the Lord, the righteous Judge, will give me on the day of his return. And the prize is not just for me but for all who eagerly look forward to his appearing.

Genesis 5:24 WEB

Enoch walked with God, and he was not found, for God took him.

2 Kings 2:11

And as they still went on and talked, behold, chariots of fire and horses of fire separated the two of them. And Elijah went up by a whirlwind into heaven.

1 Corinthians 15:51-52 NLT

But let me reveal to you a wonderful secret. We will not all die, but we will all be transformed! 52It will happen in a moment, in the blink of an eye, when the last trumpet is blown. For when the trumpet sounds, those who have died will be raised to live forever. And we who are living will also be transformed.

1 Thessalonians 4:16-17

For the Lord himself will descend from heaven with a cry of command, with the voice of an archangel, and with the sound of the trumpet of God. And the dead in Christ will rise first. 17Then we who are alive, who are left, will be caught up together with them in the clouds to meet the Lord in the air, and so we will always be with the Lord.

1 John 4:18

There is no fear in love, but perfect love casts out fear. For fear has to do with punishment, and whoever fears has not been perfected in love.

Romans 5:5 NLT

And this hope will not lead to disappointment. For we know how dearly God loves us, because he has given us the Holy Spirit to fill our hearts with his love.

GENERAL ORIENTATION FOR LEADERS

Congratulations! God has called you as a group leader for this very special course. As your fellow pilgrims work their way through this study, your ministry will be very important in helping them make smooth progress. You will probably find that as you help them to advance in their spiritual pilgrimages, you also will advance and be blessed.

To begin, here are some questions for you, as the leader, to consider:

Who? Who are the members of my group?

What? What are the needs of the members? What are my goals? What efforts will I need to make? What do others hope to receive from the study?

Where? Where am I spiritually, where do I want to go, and to where do I wish to lead this group?

How? How do I intend to encourage everyone toward reaching their goals? How do I expect this course to enrich not only the group members but also the church? How will I show appreciation to members for their efforts?

Why? Why do I believe God has called me to lead this group? Why am I (and/or my church) sponsoring this course? Why do I believe God placed these people in the group?

When? When is the best time for me to work on the study and to pray for the group?

Things expected of the leader:

Make every effort to understand the needs of your group. Seek to be a facilitator and participant. Some groups will require more leadership and teaching than others.

You should be there to keep things on track. But there are additional responsibilities:

1. **Prepare spiritually**: To lead God's pilgrims, you must be one yourself. Take your own pilgrimage seriously, letting God's Spirit work first in you. Your greatest preparation for leading your group will be to come spiritually prepared each week. Pray and seek wisdom, guidance, and empowerment for your life and leadership.
2. **Be a group participant**. Commit yourself to doing the homework each week, just like everyone else. This will give you a good grasp of the issues raised by the lessons so you can share your own insights and experiences effectively. If you do not adequately prepare, others who took the time to prepare will notice and perhaps become discouraged.
3. **Pray for your group**: You will bless the members immensely by praying for each of them regularly.

Your goals as the leader:

Your objective should be to help your fellow pilgrims remain on the narrow path to the end of their lives. You want each to become more mature in Christ, equipped, and persevering. You want each to develop deepening character, discipline, and closeness to Jesus and His people.

Organizing your group:

Size: The most effective group will be under 10 members. If you have more than this, you might consider dividing into two groups.

Gender: This is not a gender-specific study. If a group has both men and women, consider dividing during prayer.

Place:. You want this to be a comfortable experience, so find a place where you can interact in a relaxed way. If you meet in a home, have children cared for elsewhere. Sit in a circle or around a table so everyone can see each other and communicate easily.

Time: Ninety minutes works well for most studies, providing time for discussing answers and issues, sharing your lives, and praying together.

Punctuality: Start and end on time.

Refreshments: Members can decide if refreshments are served, but keep them simple so they won't become a burdensome chore or cause distraction from your study.

Assistant: You might want to choose an assistant leader to help you throughout the course – for contacting members, praying with you, filling in for you, as needed.

The suggested format for your meetings:

- Greeting and opening prayer.
- A short overview of the chapter (possibly done by an assigned volunteer for that week.)
- Review the previous week's memory verse, and read the current memory verse together.
- Let members share what particularly impacted them in this week's study.
- Move through the other questions, and be sure to encourage each other as needed.
- Share prayer needs and allow time for praying for the needs expressed.
- Close in prayer.

Before each session: Pray that God will guide you as you lead, that His presence will impact your meeting, and that each member's needs will be met. Pray for members by name, that God's Spirit will lead them into real progress in their individual pilgrimages.

The Group time:

Tips for you, personally . . .

Be a good listener. Listen intently to what participants say. Model openness, sharing your life and vulnerabilities.

Be loving and encouraging, fostering an atmosphere of safety and openness. Gently draw your group into relationship with each other.

Be flexible but firm. Keep the group on course but allow freedom for the Holy Spirit to work unexpectedly. Don't interrupt His work by rushing the time. But if someone needs in-depth counseling, suggest options and don't allow a derailing of the meeting.

.**Be sensitive**. Many of the issues raised in this study involve deeply held personal beliefs, feelings, experiences, and needs for prayer. Some things are not easy to share with others. Cultivate a safe and gracious atmosphere where members feel comfortable either sharing or not sharing. Avoid embarrassing anyone.

Be at peace: Don't get anxious if there is silence after a question. The participants may need some time to consider their responses. You don't have to jump right in, filling in the gaps. If the silence has gone on a while, you might try probing a bit or rephrasing the question.

Don't dominate. You are both a participant and facilitator. As a participant, share your answers and insights, but don't talk more than anyone else in the group. As the facilitator, you want to ask questions and give guidance.

Share humbly. You don't need to be the expert or the authority, and you don't want everyone directing all the questions and answers back to you. When someone does ask you a question that others might answer, direct it back to the group. You can say something like, "That's a good question. Do some of you have thoughts to help us with this question?"

Meeting fundamentals . . .

Hellos: Greet the members. For the first several sessions, go around the circle and let people introduce themselves. Keep in mind that as members open up with each other, they will become more comfortable and share on a deeper level.

Check-up: Ask how things are going, and encourage everyone to stay committed and keep working through their material.

Confidentiality: Press upon members to keep confidential the things shared

Participation: Let the group know that this is not a lecture series, and that everyone is encouraged to participate in the discussions.

Budget time: Guard the time. You want people to keep returning each week.

Involve everyone: It's important to reign in those who would dominate the talking and to provide openings for those who are shy. You want to encourage all to share what they are learning and experiencing in their pilgrimage.

Memory verse: These verses are specifically chosen to aid members in their pilgrimages, so urge members to learn the verse each week.

Teamwork: Work together as a team—discussing answers, clarifying, encouraging, and praying for one another.

Discussing questions: Most questions can be answered by half or more of the group.

Feedback: Request feedback from those you trust. You can ask how they are doing and how to improve the experience.

Rough patches:

If certain members are frequently absent, late, not prepared, unmotivated, monopolizing, argumentative, etc., pray for God's wisdom, and then talk one on one with the person(s) about your concern. Then pray together.

To avoid the group getting off on tangents, etc., talk to the group at the outset and establish some parameters you can agree on. Then hold the group accountable.

Encourage the more talkative to help quieter members become more engaged. Give eye contact to quieter members when asking a question, and ask them to read a textbox or answer a simple question to get them involved.

If a problem arises that you do not know how to deal with, seek outside help from your pastor or another mature leader.

If someone asks questions neither you nor anyone else in the group can answer, just say something like, "That's a great question. I'll check that out and have an answer for you next meeting."

Finally . . .

May our glorious King bless you in your service. May He grant you great joy and encouragement in leading your group through this course. He is with you and for you, and He is faithful! *Commit your way to the Lord; trust in Him, and He will act* (Psalm 37:5).

"PROGRESSING TOGETHER" LEADER'S GUIDE FOR GROUP DISCUSSIONS

CHAPTER 1

- Open in prayer
- Discuss why you have chosen to participate in this study.
- Before discussing the story, you can review together the concept of pilgrimage described in the introduction.
- **Review:** Appoint a volunteer to give a short summary of the chapter.

1. Take several minutes to discuss things that particularly impacted you in your study this week.
2. Do you believe "running" from friends and family is a common dilemma for those choosing Christ? Can you cite examples either from your life or from the lives of others?
3. Once Christian began his pilgrimage, he was so caught up with the glories awaiting him in heaven that his face shone as he described them. Discuss your answers to question #15.
4. Can you relate to the trial in the Slough of Despond? Discuss your answers to question #21.
5. There are many things that can incite fear and instability in our hearts today. From question #22, share "steps" (Bible promises) that help keep you on firm footing.

   Close in prayer: Briefly share prayer requests. Include any that this chapter may have awakened in you, as well as any others on your heart. Pray for each other and for those suffering as God's pilgrims in this world. Be sure to thank God for your Christian pilgrimages. Remember, your King is faithful!

CHAPTER 2

- Open in prayer.
- **Review:** Appoint a volunteer to give a short summary of the chapter.

1. Take several minutes to discuss things that particularly impacted you in your study this week.
2. Discuss the influence of worldly wisdom on you. How does worldly thinking gain power within believers and churches? How can we do better at overcoming this influence? Feel free to share any insights you recorded in #10.
3. Share with each other your answers to #12.
4. Scripture warns that in the End Times people will reject sound doctrine in favor of doctrines to suit their desires. (See 2 Timothy 4:3-4.) Many churches today seem willing to opt for a looser definition of the Gospel and what it means to be Christians. Discuss how a desire for cultural acceptance plays into this and how we can overcome moves to reshape the Gospel. As you feel led, discuss

also how you and your church are doing at handling the Scriptures – learning, teaching, properly interpreting, and applying them. Do you see ways to improve?

5. Share with each other some of your heroes from #19.

Close in prayer: Briefly share prayer requests. Include any that this chapter may have awakened in you, as well as any others on your heart. Pray for each other. Also, pray for the evangelists in the world and for those who need them. Be sure to thank God for your Christian pilgrimages. Remember, your King is faithful!

CHAPTER 3

- Open in prayer
- **Review:** Appoint a volunteer to give a short summary of the chapter.

1. Take several minutes to discuss things that particularly impacted you in your study this week.
2. The Holy Spirit gave Christian certain revelations suited to his pilgrimage. Referring to the "To Begin" question, share any special revelations He has given you which have become dear to you in your own pilgrimages.
3. Discuss your answers to #19. Also, are you and your church helping those in the world around you to prepare for this cataclysmic event? How can you become more intentional in this mission?
4. Discuss your answers to #20.
5. As Christian left The Interpreter's House to resume his pilgrimage, The Interpreter gave him this blessing: "May the Comforter always be with you, dear Christian, to guide you in the way that leads to the City." Throughout the world, these are increasingly difficult and dangerous times for God's pilgrims. Share your spiritual struggles and pray for each other. Pray to receive the full blessing of the Holy Spirit for your individual pilgrimages. Wait a bit and listen to the Spirit. If you feel impressed to share an insight or word of encouragement, this is a great time to do it. Jot down any encouragement you receive.

Close in prayer: Briefly share prayer requests. Include any that this chapter may have awakened in you, as well as any others on your heart. Pray for each other. Be sure to thank God for the Holy Spirit's influence, and pray for more openness to Him. Remember, your King is faithful!

CHAPTER 4

- Open in prayer
- **Review:** Appoint a volunteer to give a short summary of the chapter.

1. Take several minutes to discuss things that particularly impacted you in your study this week.
2. As you feel led, a few of you share your Christian testimonies – your encounter at the Cross. If any of you feel uncertain about your relationship with Christ, be sure to share this and receive ministry from each other. (Others who don't share their testimonies today will have an opportunity to do so next week.)
3. Share with each other your answers to question #3.
4. What did you think of the lesson about watchfulness presented in this chapter? We can walk down most streets at night and see rooms lit up by TVs. So many are watching, while so few are watchful. It's easy to appear awake but be in a deep spiritual slumber. How can we keep alert in this day and age?
5. Discuss your thoughts and experiences related to the Hill Difficulty. Do you feel prepared to head up the Hill? Do you have advice to offer each other from your answers to question #15?
6. Read Philippians 3:8-14 together and discuss your answers to question #20.

Close in prayer: Briefly share prayer requests. Include any that this chapter may have awakened in you, as well as any others on your heart. Pray for each other to keep moving forward with courage and resolve. Be sure to thank God for your Christian pilgrimages. Remember, your King is faithful!

CHAPTER 5

- Open in prayer.
- **Review:** Appoint a volunteer to give a short summary of the chapter.

1. Take several minutes to discuss things that particularly impacted you in your study this week.
2. Christian gets to share his testimony at length with other believers. Sharing our stories for mutual edification is a key part of genuine fellowship. Take some time now for those who didn't share their testimony last week and would like to do so now.
3. Christian fellowship isn't always easy, but it is highly significant to living out our faith. As you feel led, discuss your answers to question #3.
4. The Study has so much to offer. Take turns describing some favorite Bible heroes and how their stories encourage your own faith. Do you also have some favorite Bible prophesies (both fulfilled and yet to be fulfilled) that you can share?
5. Read aloud 2 Corinthians 10:3-5, Romans 13:12, 1 Thessalonians 5:8, 1 Timothy 6:12, 2 Timothy 2:3-4 and 1 Peter 5:8-11. How do these Scriptures impact you? Why is the Armory important both to individuals and churches, and why do we so often tend to shy away from issues of spiritual warfare? How can we become better equipped and do better in our efforts to raise champions of faith today?

Close in prayer: Briefly share prayer requests. Include any that this chapter may have awakened in you, as well as any others on your heart. Pray for each other and for your fellowship. Be sure to thank God for your Christian pilgrimages. He is faithful!

CHAPTER 6

- Open in prayer.
- **Review**: Appoint a volunteer to give a short summary of the chapter.

1. Take several minutes to discuss things that particularly impacted you in your study this week.
2. Read 2 Corinthians 10:3-4 together (this week's memory verse). Share your answers to question #12 as you feel led. Next, think about your church. So often we try to use human resources for fighting spiritual battles. In your estimation, does your church take spiritual warfare seriously enough?
3. Share with each other your answers to question #25.
4. We all have wounds in our lives that require God's healing touch. As you feel free, discuss areas of struggle and wounding in your life that still need healing. (Remember, Apollyon wounded Christian in his head, hand, and foot). Pray for one another, inviting God to heal and restore.

Close in prayer: Briefly share prayer requests, including any that this chapter may have awakened in you, as well as any others on your heart. Pray for each other – for victory in spiritual battles and in the humbling and dark valleys. Also, pray for those who suffer persecution as God's pilgrims in this world. Be sure to thank Him for your Christian pilgrimages. Remember, your King is faithful!

CHAPTER 7

- Open in prayer.
- **Review:** Appoint a volunteer to give a short summary of the chapter.

1. Take several minutes to discuss things that particularly impacted you in your study this week.
2. Christian and Faithful had a bit of a bumpy start but quickly became dear friends. Discuss some of your most meaningful friendships and how they became mutually beneficial.
3. Faithful had no uniform approach for conquering his temptations. (See your "c" answers in questions 5-9.) Share with each other some of your victories over temptation and what worked for you.
4. As you feel free, share with each other temptations you still struggle with and want prayer for. Pray for each other; and, as you do, use your authority as a believer. Command these temptations away in Jesus' Name, and be sure to break any strongholds they may have established. They do not belong in your lives! (Of course, if there is a serious need, be sure to see a pastor.)

Close in prayer: Briefly share any additional prayer requests, including others that this chapter may have awakened in you. Pray, too, for your church and leaders to be victorious over temptation. Be sure to thank God for your Christian pilgrimages. Remember, your King is faithful!

CHAPTER 8

- Open in prayer
- **Review:** Appoint a volunteer to give a short summary of the chapter.

1. Take several minutes to discuss things that particularly impacted you in your study this week.
2. Increasingly, the culture around us looks for ways to denigrate God's people and point out the Church's flaws. This is not a time for withdrawing but for advancing. In Colossians 4:2-6, we see Paul's heart for advancing the Gospel, even in prison. He gives certain instructions that relate to our Christian witness. Examine these together.
3. Review 1 Corinthians 13:1, 4-7. Obviously, love is not a weak quality but takes strength and courage to cultivate. Discuss your answers to question #10 related to your personal lives. Also, how can this cherished quality be nurtured in homes, in fellowships, and in the world?
4. Look at James 2:17, 26. Discuss the relationship between what we believe and how we live. How can we do better as individual Christians and as the Body of Christ? If you want, you may share ideas from question #14:
5. When it comes to talking the talk vs. walking the walk, naturally, talking is easiest. Even so, speaking the truth in love has become risky in today's culture. How can we grow both in giving and receiving correction without causing needless offense and division? Discuss, too, how we can build more loving accountability with each other.

Close in prayer: Briefly share prayer requests, including any that this chapter may have awakened in you, as well as any others on your heart. Pray for each other. Be sure to thank the Lord for your Christian pilgrimages. Remember, your King is faithful!

CHAPTER 9

- Open in prayer.
- **Review:** Appoint a volunteer to give a short summary of the chapter.

1. Take several minutes to discuss things that particularly impacted you in your study this week.
2. How is our culture like Vanity Fair? Discuss the following questions and the ramifications: Should we retreat to safety by compromising our witness? Or, should we resolve to press through in active service for Christ? Do you see examples of these positions today?
3. Evangelist warned the pilgrims to expect persecution. When considering the growing hostility in our world toward true Christians, we must grapple with how much our faith means to us. Is it really worth dying for? Discuss your answers to question #8:
4. Have you ever met with opposition because of your stand for Christ? Share your experiences. Also, share any related areas of vulnerability. How can the church be a source of strength to its members?
5. Share with each other any additional valuable thoughts or insights triggered by this chapter.

Close in prayer: Briefly share prayer requests, including any that this chapter may have awakened in you, as well as any others on your heart. Pray for each other to have strength to press through the Vanity Fair around you. Also, pray for suffering and persecuted believers in our world. If there are other pressing needs, pray for these, too. Be sure to thank Him for your Christian pilgrimages. Remember, your King is faithful!

CHAPTER 10

- Open in prayer.
- **Review:** Appoint a volunteer to give a short summary of the chapter.

1. Take several minutes to discuss things that particularly impacted you in your study this week.
2. Share your answers to question #4.
3. Why is the reasoning of Mr. By-ends and his friends so appealing? Why is it dangerous to true faith? Discuss your answers to question #9.
4. Share your answers to question #21.
5. Despite all the attractions and hostilities of Vanity Fair, Hopeful had a hunger in his soul that only God could fill. That should encourage us! Consider the spiritual harvest fields in your world. Do you see them as white for harvest? Discuss this issue.

Close in prayer: Briefly share prayer requests, including any that this chapter may have awakened in you, as well as any others on your heart. Pray for each other to stay uncompromising in your faith. Also, pray for better effectiveness in reaching the "Hopefuls" of this world. Be sure to thank God for your Christian pilgrimages. Remember, your King is faithful!

CHAPTER 11

- Open in prayer.
- **Review:** Appoint a volunteer to give a short summary of the chapter.

1. Take several minutes to discuss things that particularly impacted you in your study this week.
2. Read 1 Timothy 6:3-11. Think about the silver mine and "lucre." Which verses apply to Christian and Hopeful? Which to Mr. By-ends and his friends? How does this passage and story relate to you? How do you think it applies to your friends and to those who lead you?
3. Discuss the "River of Life," and your own experiences. Did anything happen this week as you waited on the Spirit? (Refer to question #8.)

4. Discuss the danger of becoming overly comfortable, confident, or presumptuous after enjoying River-of-Life experiences. How is it possible that even a joyful time with God can become a snare to our progress?

5. Read the lyrics to "Blessed Be Your Name." What do you feel about the message as it relates to pilgrims who might want to wander into a Bypath Meadow?

6. Have you used a "key of promise" to unlock any prison doors in your life? Share your thoughts and experiences about this. (Refer to question #22.)

Close in Prayer: Briefly share prayer requests, including any that this chapter may have awakened in you, as well as any others on your heart. Pray for victory and deliverance related to any Giant Despairs and Distrusts in your lives. Pray, also, for each other to enjoy a fresh River of God experience. And, finally, pray for discernment and wisdom when facing temptations that could follow such a wonderful experience. Be sure to thank God for your Christian pilgrimages. Remember, your King is faithful!

CHAPTER 12

- Open in prayer.
- **Review:** Appoint a volunteer to give a short summary of the chapter.

1. Take several minutes to discuss things that particularly impacted you in your study this week.
2. Share your thoughts in the "To Begin" question:
3. Discuss your answers to question #4. These attributes might seem obvious for Christian leaders; however, churches often make leaders of people lacking these attributes. Why should we all strive to grow in these qualities?
4. As Christian pilgrims, we don't always have an easy time keeping our feet on the ground and our hearts in the heights. We live in a culture that seems intent on racing over Error's cliff, abandoning all Caution, and pulling us with it. How can your church, your family, and you stay on safe footing? How can you warn others of the perils? Also, are there particular dangers you listed in #8?
5. God gives us "Shepherds" as a gift to help us progress in our spiritual pilgrimages. Their calling is not easy. Share your answers to question #20. Also, discuss ways to encourage your pastoral leaders.

Close in prayer: Briefly share any additional prayer requests, including others that this chapter may have awakened in you. Pray for each other that you can tread carefully in this world--cautious yet seeing glimpses of glory ahead. And pray for your Shepherds. Be sure to thank God for your Christian pilgrimages. Remember, your King is faithful!

CHAPTER 13

- Open in prayer.
- **Review:** Appoint a volunteer to give a short summary of the chapter.

1. Take several minutes to discuss things that particularly impacted you in your study this week.
2. Have you ever struggled with any of the "three big bruisers" – Faint-heart, Mistrust, and Guilt? Discuss your answers to question #12. Also, share any victories that might be helpful to the group.
3. Discuss your answers to question #19. You can read your prayers, if you like:
4. Ignorance was unwilling to accept correction, and many are like him. Others, thankfully, are eager to learn. In what ways are your church and you mentoring the young? Do you see ways to improve?
5. Before closing, take a moment to express gratitude for your spiritual riches in Christ

Close in prayer: Briefly share any additional prayer requests, including others that this chapter may have awakened in you. Pray for each other and for grace toward weaker "Little-faiths" you may know. Be sure to thank God for your Christian pilgrimages. Remember, your King is faithful!

CHAPTER 14

- Open in prayer.
- **Review:** Appoint a volunteer to give a short summary of the chapter.

1. Take several minutes to discuss things that particularly impacted you in your study this week.
2. In question #4, we cited Matthew 24:3-4 where Jesus warns against being led astray. Discuss some of the deceptions to which you see the Church vulnerable today. What should we do about them?
3. Share with each other your experiences and feelings with respect to the Lord's discipline. (See question #9.)
4. Discuss your answers to question #13. How does the thought of making Jesus rejoice impact you? Can you think of ways you and your church might increase His joy?
5. Share with each other your thoughts about the Enchanted Ground, our vulnerabilities in this culture, and the help we can offer each other in keeping alert. (See question #19.) _

Close in prayer: Briefly share any additional prayer requests, including others that this chapter may have awakened in you. Pray for each other to maintain spiritual clarity and faithfulness. If you have friends or loved ones who have fallen into some form of deception, pray for them. Be sure to thank God for your Christian pilgrimages. Remember, your King is faithful!

CHAPTER 15

- Open in prayer.
- **Review:** Appoint a volunteer to give a short summary of the chapter.

1. Take several minutes to discuss things that particularly impacted you in your study this week.
2. When Christian and Faithful entered Vanity Fair and provided their stirring witness, Hopeful had to make a choice: Would he follow the truth or continue to live a lie? Do you believe the Church in our day adequately carries out her task to share and exhibit God's truth? Discuss this and also your answers to question #5.
3. Refer to question #13 to discuss your journeys to understanding God's grace in your lives.
4. Hopeful was stirred from his sluggishness by reflecting on his former zeal for Christ. He remembered how Christ had given His best for him and how, in turn, he had wanted to give his best for Christ. Discuss the two Scriptures in question #22. How might you help stir in each other a first-love passion for Jesus?
5. Spend some time reflecting on Christ's greatness and goodness. As you feel free, share your prayers in question #23.

Close in prayer: Briefly share any additional prayer requests, including others that this chapter may have awakened in you. Pray for each other and for your witness to unbelievers. Be sure to thank God for your Christian pilgrimages. Remember, your King is faithful!

CHAPTER 16

- Open in prayer.
- **Review:** Appoint a volunteer to give a short summary of the chapter.

1. Take several minutes to discuss things that particularly impacted you in your study this week.
2. Discuss your answers to question #3 related to the role accountability plays in a well-conducted pilgrimage.
3. Many views of salvation are carefully nuanced to sound legitimate when they are not. While seeming to espouse the Gospel, they actually subvert it. Discuss the two formulas for salvation below. Ignorance holds to one, and Christian holds to the other. Which is valid?
   - My good works + Christ's sacrifice = my justification and salvation
   - Christ's goodness + Christ's sacrifice = my justification and salvation

4. Confer with each other about how best to present the Gospel to seekers with clarity and integrity. Share any useful Scriptures.
5. Consider together the issue of backsliding:
   - Do you know someone who is backsliding? How does James 5:19-20 address this, and how does it make you feel to have an opportunity to change eternal destinies?

- Do you agree with the progression of backsliding in question #22? Feel free to share your answers to question #23.

Close in Prayer: Pray for the needs expressed in both parts of the last question. Briefly share any other prayer requests, including any that this chapter may have awakened in you, as well as any others on your heart. Pray for God's people to stand with His truth and not be confused by "Ignorance" beliefs. Be sure to thank God for your Christian pilgrimages. Remember, your King is faithful!

CHAPTER 17

- Open in prayer.
- **Review:** Appoint a volunteer to give a short summary of the chapter.

1. Take several minutes to discuss things that particularly impacted you in your study this week.
2. Look at the Scriptures in question #3 and your answers. What encouragement does this offer as you look ahead at your pilgrimage?
3. In questions #16 and #17, we see Christian terrified and Hopeful full of hope. Look at these questions and answers. Celebrate that we are all unique with various gifts for helping each other. Point out some of the qualities you appreciate in each other.
4. Discuss your answers to question #4 about God's joy over you. As you consider heaven, how do Jesus' words in Matthew 25:21 impact you? ("His master said to him, 'Well done, good and faithful servant. You have been faithful over a little; I will set you over much. Enter into the joy of your master.'")
5. There's such joy ahead! Review some of your answers to questions #19 and 20 and how these inspire you.
6. Share your thoughts about Pastor Edward Payson's Letter to His Sister (#26).

Close in prayer: Briefly share prayer requests. Include any that this chapter may have awakened in you, as well as any others on your heart. Pray for those like Ignorance, who are on a false pilgrimage. Pray for each other never to forget the lessons of this story and to finish your pilgrimages victoriously. Be sure to thank God for your Christian pilgrimages. Remember, your King is faithful!

OPTIONAL FOR NEXT WEEK: Congratulations! You deserve a celebration, so let's have one! This week take some time to review and reflect on the entire study. Be prepared to share what this course has meant to you, any ways it has impacted you, or any changes you have made in your life.

Optional Celebration Meeting:

Enjoy food and fellowship. Be sure to include this one final "Progressing Together."

1. John Bunyan's "The Author's Defense of His Book" precedes his classic story. Read the excerpt below. Do you believe Bunyan succeeded in his mission?
2. Share what this study has meant to you and how it has impacted you. Also, state any changes you have made in your life as a result of this study.
3. Discuss together some of your favorite parts of *The Pilgrim's Progress* story.
4. As your time together in this study ends, consider how you can be a source of ongoing support to each other in your Christian pilgrimages.

Close in prayer: Take the time to lay hands on the members of your group, one at a time, praying for God's grace, joy, and progress over their pilgrimage. What a powerful blessing that will be! Let prayers, congratulatory hugs, and tears of joy abound! Congratulations, you made it!

Excerpt from "The Author's Defense of His Book"

My mysteries and shadow, indeed do hold
The truth, as cabinets enclose the gold.
The prophets used metaphors much to serve
To set forth truth: yes, any who observe
Christ, His apostles too, shall plainly see
That truths to this day in such cloaks will be.
And now, before I put away my pen,
I'll show the profit of my book; and then
Commit both you and it into the Hand
That pulls the strong down, and makes weak ones stand.
This book lays out before your very eyes
The man who seeks the everlasting prize:
Where he's from and where he's going are both shown
What he does and leaves undone are both made known:
It also shows you how he runs and runs
Until to the gate of glory he comes.
Also are the ones who in haste would life gain,
Seeming like the lasting crown they'd attain:
Here also you may see the reason why
They lose their labor, and like fools they die.
This book will make a traveler of you
If by its counsel you'll learn what to do;
It will direct you to the Holy Land,
If its directions you will understand:
It will cause the slothful to active be;
Also the blind will delightful things see.
Are you for something rare and profitable?
Would you like to see truth found in a fable?
Are you forgetful? Would you like to remember
From New Year's Day to the last of December?
Then read my thoughts, and they will stick like burrs,
And may be to the helpless, sure comforters.
This book is written in such dialect,
As may the minds of listless men affect:

It seems a novelty, and yet contains
Nothing but sound and honest gospel strains.
Would you divert yourself from melancholy?
Would you be peaceful, yet be far from folly?
Would you read riddles and their explanation?
Or else be drowned in your contemplation?
Do you love picking at meat? Or would you view
A man in the clouds, and hear him speak to you?
Would you be in a dream, and yet not sleep?
Or would you in a moment laugh and weep?
Would you lose yourself and meet nothing tragic,
And find yourself again without using magic?
Would you read yourself, and read you know not what,
And yet know whether you are blessed or not,
By reading the same lines? Oh then, come, draw near,
Lay my book, your head, and heart together here.

ANSWER KEY

CHAPTER 1

TO BEGIN
(Your answer)

DRAWN TO THE PILGRIMAGE
1. The lost world; lost sinners
2. The burden of his sins
3. The Bible; it convicted him and made him miserable in his sins. Hebrews 4:12 says God's Word is alive and sharp, piercing deeply into our thoughts and motives.
4. David said that before he confessed his sins, his body wasted away and his strength dried up; he said that after he came clean and confessed his sins to God, he experienced forgiveness and was blessed. If we do not feel peace in our lives, perhaps there's sin we need to surrender to God.
5. (Your answer)

EVANGELIST APPEARS
6. Someone who faithfully delivers the message of Good News. Evangelist in the story pointed him away from the City of Destruction and toward the way of salvation.
7. (Your answer)

PURSUED BY OBSTINATE AND PLIABLE
8. a. Thinking he had lost his mind, they lost patience with him quickly and began to persecute him. He must not let them keep him from eternal life. b. God's pilgrims must not love family more than Christ; He calls us to take up our cross and leave our families, if need be, for His sake.
9. (Your answer)
10. Obstinate. Rejecting God's Word as ridiculous, he resorted to scoffing and insults.
11. (Your answer)
12. He seems to have an open heart to salvation and is willing to leave on a pilgrimage. However, after his first serious trial, he gives up and runs home. While Christian bears a burden that represents conviction of sin, Pliable carries none. Thus, he is more prone to emotional whims.
13. (Your answer)
14. (Your answer)

CHRISTIAN AND PLIABLE DISCUSS HEAVENLY THINGS
15. (Your answer)

THE SLOUGH OF DESPOND AND HELP
16. While both struggled to get out of the Slough, Pliable struggled toward his home in the City of Destruction and returned there. Christian, on the other hand, struggled toward his goal and received God's Help.
17. (Your answer)
18. He fled the fear that pursued him and fell in.
19. God's promises. These promises enable us to partake of God's character and escape the world's corruption. (Note: Bunyan identifies the steps as "The Promises" in the story's sidebar.)
20. That whatever promises God has made in Scripture, Christ fulfilled them all. Each is reliable, and we can stand on them. When we say, "Amen," we say it confidently, and to God's glory.
21. (Your answer)
22. (Your answer

CHAPTER 2

TO BEGIN
(Your answer)

CHRISTIAN MEETS WORLDLY-WISEMAN
1. Carnality; guided by the sinful nature.
2. They will be accursed.
3. Fierce wolves who will come from within our own circles to draw us away from the true path. Stay alert and on guard against them.
4. (Your answer)
5. Morality: man-centered, works-based religion; Legality: Those who promote justification by their own good deeds; Civility: Those who promote benevolent behavior as the solution to their sin problem.
6. He is a seducing false prophet. He represents those who are guided by the values of worldly temporal wisdom and who reject the true wisdom that comes from God. He advocates a "works-righteousness" where one attains salvation by being morally upright and obeying rules. But the Old Covenant, represented by Mt. Sinai, is superseded by Christ's New Covenant.
7. (Your answer)
8. Mt. Sinai, representing the weight of the Law of Moses, threatened to crush him. The guilt he feels becomes all the more oppressive.
9. Our own righteousness is as filthy rags to God.
10. (Your answer)

EVANGELIST DELIVERS CHRISTIAN FROM ERROR
11. Christian allowed himself to be led astray and stepped completely out of God's will.
12. Evangelist wasn't interested in soothing Christian's stricken conscience before he had fully repented. He was more interested in delivering him from death. These Scriptures were truth.
13. (Your answer)
14. a. Turning Christian out of the Way b. trying to make the Cross repulsive to him
    c. directing him to a path that leads to death.
15. Because there is no other way for us to be saved except through Christ. We are saved only by faith, and those who rely on legalism are actually under a curse.
16. (Your answer)
17. (Your answer)

CHRISTIAN IS FORGIVEN
18. Good news of grace, forgiveness, and hope.
19. (Your answer)

CHAPTER 3

TO BEGIN
(Your answer)

CHRISTIAN MEETS GOOD-WILL AND ENTERS THE GATE
1. Christ said the gate to life is narrow, the sense being that it is difficult to enter. The wide gate, on the other hand, is kinder to the sinful nature and attractive to the masses.
2. The devil, of course, will try to thwart seekers from entering the way to life.
3. He gladly opened the gate to Christian and helped him in; accepted Christian, despite his flaws; he directed him onto the pilgrim's path and to the Interpreter's House.

THE INTERPRETER'S HOUSE

4. The name Interpreter represents the Holy Spirit well since He is the One who helps by interpreting God's truth to honest seekers. In a world where we are so prone to deception, we need the Spirit's guidance.

5. (Your answer)

THE MAN IN THE PICTURE

6. He is a faithful minister of the Gospel. The picture exhibits the traits that pastors, spiritual fathers, elders, and mentors should exhibit. As authentic under-shepherds to Christ, these alone have authority to guide pilgrims.

7. This portrait expresses things to look for in a spiritual guide so we won't be fooled by an imposter. If we want to discern between authentic and counterfeit ministers, and if we would be authentic, it is good to study this kind of model intently.

8. a. His eyes are directed to heaven. (His eyes are fixed on Jesus and the heavenly realm.) b. The Bible is in his hand. (He is committed to God's Word, not to his own opinion.) c. The law of truth is on his lips. (He is committed to speaking God's truth alone to turn himself and others from sin.) d. The world is behind his back. (He so loves the Lord that the world neither allures nor encumbers him.) e. He pleads with people. (He knows eternal souls are at stake and urges people to come to salvation.) f. He wears a golden crown. (He lives for the glorious reward that awaits him in heaven.)

THE ROOM FILLED WITH DUST

9. This represents the important work of grace called sanctification. The Law "raises the dust," but the Gospel, like the sprinkling of water, enables a purifying work in the heart.

PASSION AND PATIENCE

10. *Passion*: those who are driven by insatiable carnal appetites and lose in the end. *Patience*: those who have an eye for "the best things" – heaven's reward – and are willing to wait for them.

11. (Your answer)

12. (Your answer)

THE FIRE BY THE WALL

13. The devil tries to extinguish the fire ignited in our hearts through salvation, but God pours the oil of His grace on the flames. No matter how bad things get, our hearts still burn with love for God because of grace.

THE BEAUTIFUL (STATELY) PALACE

14. Fear of armed guards blocking the entrance stopped all but one from trying. The one exception was a man of resolute purpose who fought his way through and overcame all resistance.

15. They urged them to continue in the faith despite the many tribulations that accompany entering the kingdom of God.

16. Many want eternal life but lack the will to face the persecution that comes with it. True believers must have a burning passion to fight the good fight of faith. They know it is worth it in the end

THE MAN IN THE IRON CAGE

17. The tragedy of those who fall away. As long as the man believes he cannot be restored, he feels no hope of salvation. Thus, he does not pray or turn to God, and he keeps his distance from God. We should consider this when we start to slip away.

18. The Scriptures tell us to use gentleness when correcting those who have strayed.

19. (Your answer)

THE MAN WITH THE TERRIFYING DREAM

20. (Your answer)

21. (Your answer)

CHAPTER 4

TO BEGIN

(Your answer)

CHRISTIAN REACHES THE CROSS

1. He came to the Cross and trusted Christ's finished work there. The burden fell off and rolled down into a grave.
2. This signifies that his burden of guilt is gone permanently. He is forgiven!
3. (Your answer)
4. These three represent the three Persons of the Triune God. The Father announces that Christian's sins are forgiven; the Son strips him of his sinful garments and dresses him in garments of righteousness; and the Holy Spirit marks his forehead with a seal of his salvation and gives him a scroll. The scroll reminds him of his salvation and assures him of immediate entrance at the Gate.
5. We come to Christ in filthy garments stained with sin. God doesn't clean up those old garments. Rather, He discards them and gives us brand new "garments" – the best He has.
6. The seal is the Holy Spirit. He guarantees our inheritance in heaven, and He is God's stamp of ownership.

FALSE CHRISTIANS ALONG THE WAY

7. Simple, Sloth, and Presumption. These three are off the Way and sleeping with fetters. Simple is unwise and won't heed godly advice, Sloth is too lazy to take heed, and Presumption thinks he needs no help at all. Each represents a form of religious indifference, and all brush aside correction.
8. He did not take the Lord seriously but fell asleep; he disowned Jesus and was grief-stricken; we must stay alert in order to avoid serious failures.
9. To keep watchful. This is how to avoid deception and temptation.
10. (Your answer)
11. They came onto the Way, but they came in a forbidden manner; they didn't read the Book; they escaped carrying a burden; they avoided the Wicket Gate and the Cross; and they are seeking praise. For his part, Christian has his coat, the mark on his forehead, and his scroll.
12. Formality represents those who practice religious rituals without true faith, and Hypocrisy represents pretenders without true faith.
13. God has a prescribed way to salvation. To come in another way ignores Christ's Lordship. In these end times, many are writing their own rules and fashioning their own religion. Christ is the gate through which we must enter, and only those who obey Him can hope for eternal life.

THREE WAYS FROM WHICH TO CHOOSE

14. One led straight up the hill, and the other two went to the right and to the left. The difficult one is a proving ground of a believer's sincerity. The Christian walk requires sacrifice, self-denial, and discipline. It can mean emotional turmoil and lost friendships, even persecution.
15. (Your answer)

CHRISTIAN LOSES HIS SCROLL AT THE PLEASANT ARBOR

16. Perhaps a mountain retreat the Lord provides. We get away from it all for a bit and don't want to go home. In such a place, it's easy to give up vigilance, get sleepy, and presume a bit too much.

RESPONDING TO FEAR

17. (Your answer)

RECOVERING THE SCROLL

18. He slept, he grew alarmed that he slept, Mistrust and Timorous frightened him, and he had to go backward. Upon realizing his loss, he fell under condemnation. He returned to the Arbor and reclaimed his scroll.

FACING LIONS IN THE WAY

19. Fear of fellowship. There are many reasons people fear openly joining other believers in true Christian fellowship. Joining a church makes one's profession public, and that can be scary. At Watchful's urging, Christian faced his fear and found that things weren't as bad as they appeared. The lions were, indeed, bound.
20. (Your answer)

CHAPTER 5

TO BEGIN

(Your answer)

RECEIVED AT THE PALACE BEAUTIFUL

1. Watchful represents a vigilant pastor who keeps watch over his flock's souls. He helped Christian get past his fears, but he must also interview people to determine their legitimacy.
2. Both imposters and authentic believers might seek entrance into the fellowship. Some imposters can mean the church harm. Churches should be hospitable but also well-guarded. Membership should never be automatic.
3. (Your answer)
4. *Discretion*: ability to decide responsibly, circumspect or heedful of potential consequences. *Prudence*: indicates wisdom applied to practice -- practically wise, careful, discreet. *Piety*: Reverence for God and love of His character; loving His will and zealous devotion to serving Him. *Charity*: an attitude of heart that moves people to think favorably of others, to love and do them good.
5. True Christian fellowship builds believers up as they share their faith and experiences together. Too often we reduce our fellowship times to having fun together. While fun can be good, it is substandard Christian fellowship if it becomes our steady diet.
6. The Lord's Supper is more than a memorial, and it is no casual matter. It is a deeply enriching fellowship experience, a communion. Members sit down and dine together, feasting sumptuously, reflecting late into the night, sharing in depth about the Lord and all He means to them, and committing their lives into His keeping.

THE ROOM CALLED PEACE

7. Christian's profession of faith was validated, he was invited into the fellowship of believers, and he enjoyed a rich time of communion with Christ and his people. All this so nurtured his mind and soul that he felt complete rest.
8. He found peace with God at the Cross. The peace of God is another peace, a state of inner harmony. It involves resting in one's faith, enjoying assurance that God is in control. Christian had just come through a season of difficulty alone. Fellowship in the Palace helped him immensely. Life is hard in this world. Enjoying peace is a wonderful blessing.
9. (Your answer)

THE STUDY AND THE ARMORY

10. Participation in Bible study. Reading and meditating on God's Word and all His wonderful works is a great way to start the day.
11. Paul commanded Timothy to study Scripture so he could interpret and communicate it properly. In the modern Church, a dramatic erosion of faith in Scriptural authority has too often occurred. Complacency toward God's Word hinders our understanding and transformation. Increasingly, we become conformed to our fallen culture and powerless to change it.
12. (Your answer)
13. The pilgrim may not yet be fully aware, but he will find battles that require armor. An armory is an arsenal where weapons are kept. This Scripture speaks of putting on the "full armor of God," which includes various pieces to assure victory.

14. Scripture makes it clear that this world is a battlefield, and Christians are in a war against hostile enemy forces that hate God's truth. Without proper equipping, we can become casualties, unable to be victorious for Christ. Christian's friends took him to the Armory first to educate him and then to equip him.

15. We should take comfort that He uses ordinary implements within our reach, not spectacular things beyond us. Also, He uses simple people with faith to confound the wise and powerful of this world. We should not get hung up on fancy resources. We should pick up what God provides and use it in faith, remembering that He is our Source and strength.

THE DELECTABLE MOUNTAINS AND RESUMING THE JOURNEY

16. These mountains offer a sense of perspective when we are down in the trenches. Off in the distance, they seem to represent distinct views of the blessings and privileges that are attainable in this life through perseverance.

17. Believers, especially young ones, can *feel* prepared to run out and conquer the world. But they need training. Much of that training comes by way of humbling experiences. Paul was well seasoned but still needed his "thorn" to keep him humble.

18. (Your answer)

CHAPTER 6

TO BEGIN

(Your answer)

THE VALLEY OF HUMILIATION AND APOLLYON

1. (Your answer)
2. To humble and test them. He wanted them never to forget their need for reliance on Him. There was a great danger that their blessings would lead to pride and subsequent destruction.
3. To destroy Christian's soul.
4. He intimidates, bribes, reasons, and uses guilt. He begins by identifying himself as Christian's master. Then, he promises to give Christian whatever he wants if he'll return. Next, he points to others who forsake their pilgrimage. He promises things will go well if Christian will do likewise. He then projects himself as a forgiving sovereign. He speaks of the terrible plight of Christ's followers and the shame they suffer. He impugns Christ for not delivering them. He then condemns Christian, citing the sins and failures that would make him an unacceptable pilgrim. All this is to convince Christian to return to the City of Destruction.
5. Against Christ: He contends that these trials are tests of a pilgrim's love and endurance; and that they will bring great glory later. Against Christian: Concerning his own failure, Christian appeals to his King's merciful and forgiving nature. He asserts that he has been pardoned.

THE INEVITABLE CONFLICT

6. He wants to scare Christian into thinking he is invincible and that the way is now impassable. Today, the devil can defeat us by making us feel he has blocked our way, the Lord has forsaken us, and that we have no reason to go on.

7. The Christian life involves spiritual warfare. This world is a battleground, and we need to take this reality seriously. God often allows conflicts in our lives to humble and refine us, but He also uses them to train us to win our battles. Christian must learn to stand against the demon confronting him.

8. There is no way of escape, for Christian has no armor on his backside. The only way to test his armor's strength is to face his enemy. It is the same for us. The easy way may prove the deadliest.

9. *Hand*: Christian cannot wield his sword effectively. Perhaps his faith is so wounded that he has trouble using God's promises for either offensive or defensive purposes. *Foot*: He can no longer walk wisely. Because these shoes represent the Gospel of peace, his stumbling affects his conduct and ability to be an effective witness.

10. Our spiritual battles are not always light skirmishes. They can be quite enduring and wearying to our resolve. In those times, the armor is all the more important. We can become so harassed, however, that we lose our chief weapon and feel we have lost.

11. (Your answer)
12. (Your answer)
13. This one instance records Jesus using Scripture three times to resist the devil's temptations.
14. (Your answer)

HEALING

15. God provided him leaves from the Tree of Life. These leaves represent renewed spiritual life from trusting God. He took hold of them and applied them to his wounds. These healed the wounds to his head, hand, and feet. His related sins were forgiven and his mistakes corrected. Also, his soul was restored and his strength renewed.
16. No! He learned the value of his sword. He resumes his journey, keeping his sword drawn and ready for wielding the truth of God's Word.

THE VALLEY OF THE SHADOW OF DEATH

17. The only way to the Celestial City, very solitary, a wilderness with deserts and pits, drought, very hard to pass through. For us, this can be a period of spiritual distress and depression. In this state, we can feel abandoned and that God is no longer in control. Deep darkness is not death, but it sure can seem like it.
18. Only Christians have known the comfort of God's presence and the thrill of His provision and victory. Now, however, it seems He has withdrawn completely. But all is not as it appears. If we trust God, we can come through this terrible place with deeper maturity and increased faith.
19. God's people had already seen God do so many miracles on their behalf. Nevertheless, the report of the faithless spies demoralized them and filled them with fear. Abandoning the voices of faith and courage, they wanted to turn back to Egypt. Christian hears a similar terrifying account but chooses to press on. While perhaps not so overt, many voices in our culture attempt to dissuade us from making a faithful Christian pilgrimage.
20. *Ditch*: As with the Pharisees, this is presumptuously adhering to false security derived from legalism and self-righteousness; *Quagmire*: This is the opposite problem. After falling into some sin, this is a crisis of faith that leaves one despairing of God's mercy. *Safe place:* Keep to the center of the way. The narrowness indicates the extreme caution one must exercise in the face of these two dangerous threats.
21. Demons are the blasphemers. They like to exploit our vulnerabilities by feeding us their lies and weakening our faith. They know that if they confuse us, making us think the dark thoughts are our own, that we will lose hope.
22. Christian is in a furnace of affliction that makes him feel doomed to Hell. Having lost confidence in his sword, he cries out in agonizing prayer and keeps praying. He also makes a faith declaration that he will not turn back. He stays the course.
23. This can represent many inner conflicts – fears; depression and oppression; lack of peace; mental, emotional and spiritual turmoil; feelings of doubt and defeat; and feelings of God being distant and uncaring.
24. First, it meant he wasn't really alone and that other pilgrims were going through this trial, too. Second, he realized that, according to the promise, God truly was with him. Third, he had hope that he could find fellowship there. Finally, daybreak came. He could now see everything more clearly as he passed through the Valley.
25. (Your answer)

CHAPTER 7

TO BEGIN

(Your answer)

CHRISTIAN AND FAITHFUL MEET IN THE WAY

1. Christian runs to catch up with Faithful but then runs past him. His pride stirred again, he overestimates his own spirituality and takes a humiliating tumble. Unable to get back on his feet again, he must rely upon help from the one he underestimated. Prov. 16:18 warns that pride and arrogance result in a destructive fall.

2. The two became close friends. We cannot enjoy harmonious fellowship when we lag behind or run ahead of each other. We must walk together humbly and support one another.

NEWS FROM HOME
3. They discussed the claims that their City would be judged. Some spoke derisively of Christian, however, and only Faithful feared the danger enough to leave.
4. Many took note of his testimony and discussed the alarm he sounded. It looked like no one really listened; but seeds were planted, and Faithful became convinced to embark on his own pilgrimage.

FAITHFUL'S CONFRONTATIONS WITH TEMPTATION
5. a. Wanton b. She is a seductive woman who tempts Faithful to immoral gratification of the flesh. c. He remembered an old writing that warned him. He shut his eyes and moved on. d. (Your answer)
6. a. The Old Man (Adam the First) b. He is a persuasive old guy from Deceit. He offers Faithful great wages simply to enjoy himself. He also offers Faithful an inheritance of all he owns and his three daughters (Lust of the Flesh, Lust of the Eyes, and Pride of Life) in marriage. c. Faithful saw a Scripture about putting off the Old Man (Eph. 4:22) and realized this man wanted to enslave him. Faithful stopped their talk, resisted insults, steered away, admitted his weakness, and moved forward. d. (Your answer)
7. a. Moses – Representing the Law (legalism) b. He unmercifully pummeled Faithful with feelings of guilt for his inclinations toward Adam the First. He offers nothing but beatings. c. In this case, the pilgrim cannot resist. The Lord, Himself, extends grace and orders Moses to stop. d. (Your answer) e. The law and commandment is holy and good. He is so grateful that God, through Christ, rescued this once wretched person and that now he lives without condemnation.
8. a. Discontent b. This one seeks to convince Faithful that the Way is dishonorable and that it will offend many prominent friends and relatives. He offers escape from causing such an offense. c. Faithful responds that he has already parted company with these "friends" and that he has no interest in their opinion. He quotes Scriptures that validate humility. d. (Your answer)
9. a. Shame b. This one was bold, accusatory, and convincing. His string of accusations demeans Faithful, his faith, and all pilgrims. Shame wants to get Faithful to escape the dishonor of the pilgrimage. c. Faithful thought of Scripture. He also considered how God's Word, not the world's opinion, would lead to life. He forcefully commanded Shame to leave him but had to persist as Shame didn't leave immediately. d. (Your answer)

A PERSONAL LOOK AT TEMPTATION
10. There are no spiritual cookie cutters when it comes to faith. We are individuals with particular strengths and vulnerabilities. The devil understands this and plans his attacks against us accordingly
11. (Your answer)
12. (Your answer)
13. (Your answer)
14. (Your answer)

CHAPTER 8
TO BEGIN
(Your answer)

FAITHFUL AND TALKATIVE
1. That he might prefer talking the talk over walking the walk; that engaging in theological discussions might interest him far more than the pilgrimage does.
2. That profiting spiritually should always be our primary goal.

CHRISTIAN AND FAITHFUL DISCUSS TALKATIVE

3. We are responsible not to let others deceive us. As "children of light," our call is to overcome and expose darkness. In these evil days, we must walk carefully, relying on God's Spirit to reveal to us goodness and truth. We must understand God's will.

4. He says he has proof of Talkative's guilt and that people of character feel similarly.

5. Talkative loves putting on a show for those who don't know him but exhibits ugliness at home where people do know him. He doesn't pray, he fails to repent, he is unjust and deceitful, and he leads his family astray.

6. We can recognize false prophets because they don't bear good (godly) fruit. Just as we recognize healthy and diseased trees by their fruit, so we recognize spiritually healthy and unhealthy people by the good or bad fruit they produce.

7. The body without the soul is a dead carcass; and words without deeds are dead, too. The soul of true faith is the part that puts it into practice and bears fruit.

8. God's grace saves us. It is a gift that cannot be earned. Nevertheless, God intends to do a work that enables us to produce good works for His glory.

9. He makes a lot of noise but has no real substance. Without genuine faith, he becomes quite annoying with his talking.

10. (Your answer)

FAITHFUL CONFRONTS TALKATIVE'S ERROR

11. a. Through a great outcry against sin. b. Great knowledge of Gospel mysteries.

12. Hypocrites can say all kinds of things against sin and still playact. Those who truly loathe sin will resist it.

13. Because too many people who profess faith fill themselves with head knowledge that never leads to true transformation. Knowledge of value is the kind that moves a person to faith, obedience, and love from the heart.

14. (Your answer)

15. a. It shows itself to the one who possesses it through conviction of sin, repentance, submission to Christ, and a changed life b. Observers see it, first, through a public confession of Christ. They see it, second, in a lifestyle change consistent with a confession of faith.

16. (Your answer)

TALKATIVE CHOOSES TO PART COMPANY

17. Those with bad character are happy to pull us into their sin and corrupt our good moral character.

18. He was faithful to share the truth honestly and straightforwardly. If Talkative perishes, it won't be due to Faithful's failure. Faithful's conscience is clear.

19. This will either force them to receive correction and repent; or it will force them to leave. Of course, these are the two alternatives that will enrich and not corrupt the church. Religious hypocrites allowed to fit comfortably within the church bring corruption that even those who are worldly notice.

20. The world will judge us all to be hypocrites. The Scripture clearly expresses that we must live what we profess. When we do not, unbelievers devalue God's Word because of us.

21. We should also be an example by the way we live – in our conduct, love, faith, and purity.

22. (Your answer)

CHAPTER 9

TO BEGIN

(Your answer)

EVANGELIST ENCOURAGES THE PILGRIMS

1. In spite of their weaknesses, they had persevered in their pilgrimage.

2. Not to become weary in well-doing, to run in such a way to get the prize, to go into strict training, not to let anyone seize their crown, to hold on to what they already have, to beware of the devil, to let the kingdom be uppermost in their minds, to believe unflinchingly in the things that are unseen, to guard their hearts

and let nothing of this world get in and corrupt them, to set their faces like flint. He tells them not to forget they have the power of Heaven and earth on their side. God is with them.

3. An alien and stranger. No. Hatred and persecution

4. Jesus is coming soon. Don't let anyone steal our crown. Because Jesus is coming soon and life is short, we must be diligent. God will reward a faithful Christian with an eternal crown. But we also have enemies who would sabotage our gains and steal our crown. To win and keep our crown, we must cautiously guard our progress, watching carefully not to let anyone move in, steer us the wrong way, and seize our reward. Christ's return is sooner than ever!

5. (Your Answer)

6. Because God has proven Himself faithful, Isaiah can make a firm resolve to move forward in faith. Likewise, Paul declares he won't look backwards but will firmly go forward, pressing on to his goal. He urges us not to let our own progress slip away.

7. The pilgrims will face extreme hardships – enemies will persecute them, and one will die. They must be faithful and persevere to the end. They need to remember in their suffering the Scripture that urges them to commit everything to their faithful Creator and continue to do good.

8. (Your answer)

9. We tend to think that being blessed means we won't suffer.

VANITY FAIR

10. Jesus honored the Word of God and wielded it against the tempter. Jesus resisted pride, and we should also. We should not take the devil's bait. Christ's allegiance was such that nothing the world offered would divert Him from honoring God and completing His mission. This should be our commitment, as well.

11. a. They dressed differently (Christ's robes of righteousness). b. They spoke a different language (biblical and spiritual conversation). c. They shunned the Fair's wares (rejected worldly values and only bought something unavailable there – truth).

12. Those who walk according to the course of this world are dead in sin. They live in sinful lust and disobedience under the power of the devil. They are children of disobedience and wrath. God's people, on the other hand, are now alive – loved, saved by God's gift of grace, raised up to sit with Christ in heavenly places, and promised an amazing eternal hope and future.

13. Some cause a commotion by standing for truth and righteousness; many more do not. Persecution is rising in our land, and it is getting more difficult to sit on the fence as a cultural Christian. Biblical Christianity is under assault and so are its adherents. We see battles raging on many fronts, from theological to ideological to practical.

14. (Your answer)

15. (Your answer)

16. (Your answer)

17. (Your answer)

18. By doing things like reading and knowing God's Word, persevering in faith, making integrity a priority, seeking the Spirit of Truth, refusing to compromise with the lies around us.

19. (Your answer)

CHRISTIAN AND FAITHFUL STAND TRIAL

20. (Your answer)

21. Wonderfully! A chariot immediately transported him to heaven!

CHAPTER 10

TO BEGIN

(Your answer)

HOPEFUL JOINS CHRISTIAN

1. Hopeful. He became a pilgrim by observing how Christian and Faithful conducted themselves during their suffering. Also, he related that many more from the Fair were soon to follow.
2. (Your answer)
3. Faithful emphasizes the importance of faithfulness to the pilgrimage. Hopeful, emphasizes the importance of maintaining hopefulness. Just as our conversion experiences differ, so do our personalities. God gives us our own strengths to complement each other.
4. (Your answer)
5. They made a covenant together, vowing to be companions.

THE PILGRIMS MEET MR. BY-ENDS

6. Refined speech can cloak the truth. People can be very polite outwardly, yet sinful and self-righteous in their hearts. People need to hear the true Gospel that calls for repentance from sin.
7. Lord Turn-about (E), Lord Time-server (C), Mr. Smooth-man (A), Mr. Facing-bothways (D), Mr. Any-thing (F), Rev. Two-tongues (G), Lady Feigning (B)

MR. BY-ENDS'S RELIGION

8. a. It goes with the flow, never striving against wind or current. b. It is a religion most zealous when it is refined and elegant. It walks boldly when the sun shines on it and people applaud it.
9. (Your answer)
10. (Your answer)

THEY MUST PART COMPANY

11. To walk with true pilgrims, Mr. By-ends must go with them against the wind and current. It would mean embracing their faith, whether the path led to riches or poverty, honor or dishonor. The three cannot walk together unless Mr. By-ends embraces a true pilgrimage.

MR. BY-ENDS'S THREE FRIENDS

12. Unlike these self-serving men, Christ found His satisfaction in always doing His Father's will and in finishing His task. He purposed always to please the Father, to love Him, to do exactly what He commanded, and to glorify Him by completing His assigned mission.

THEY EVALUATE CHRISTIAN AND HOPEFUL

13. That they are rigid and dogmatic; they are lovers of their own opinions; they are willing to break fellowship with those who disagree; they are legalistic and judgmental; they are headstrong; they are unwilling to regard the weather; they are willing to risk all for God; they are committed to their ideas even if the whole world opposes them; they are willing to wear rags; and they are foolish and lack common sense.
14. They neither understand nor receive the things of the Spirit, which can only be spiritually discerned.
15. *Matthew 10:16*: Jesus says to beware of wolves, warning us to be as wise as serpents and harmless as doves. Mr. Hold-the-world twists it to mean wisdom is found in avoiding the loss of worldly possessions. *Matthew 5:45*: Jesus says God sends His rain on everyone. Mr. Hold-the-world claims that fools may choose to go through rain, but he and his kind only choose good weather. *Job 22:24*: In context, the Scripture says to lay our gold down and let God be our gold. Mr. Hold-the-world, however, takes the Scripture as a command to accumulate gold for himself.
16. Peter calls those who twist the Scriptures ignorant and unstable. Their error will destroy them.

A QUESTION FROM MR. BY-ENDS

17. Not looking for his own benefit, he sought the benefit of others that they might be saved.
18. Jesus says we cannot serve two masters. He is our Master. Trying to reconcile God's will with worldly greed is indefensible. Their natural enmity for each other, requires us either to embrace one or the other.
19. (Your answer)

CHRISTIAN ANSWERS THE QUESTION

20. The men of Fair-speech interpreted Scripture from their core value – greed. Christian interpreted Scripture from his core value – honoring Christ and the truth of His Word.
21. (Your answer)

CHAPTER 11

TO BEGIN

(Your answer)

IN THE PLAIN CALLED EASE

1. Samuel's sons, Joel and Abijah; Delilah; Elisha's servant, Gehazi; Haman; Judas. In each case, dishonest gain (lucre) was involved.
2. (Your answer)
3. (Your answer)

THE APPEAL OF DEMAS

4. Luke and Demas. Luke authored the books of Luke and Acts. Demas abandoned the ministry because he was "in love with this present world," which included the dazzling things of this world. Luke remained with Paul, probably until the end.
5. They died in the silver-mine. Jesus warns us not to lose our soul by trying to gain the world.

THE PILLAR OF LOT'S WIFE

6. They must beware. An unwary pilgrim might escape one judgment but fall to another. They must shun her sin and give attention to caution. They do not want to be her type of example.

THE RIVER OF GOD

7. They came to the delightful River of God. All believers partake of the Holy Spirit. There are times, however, when He unveils His presence and shares His blessings much more distinctly. Keeping to the pilgrim's path will eventually lead to this pleasant "River."
8. (Your answer)

TEMPTATION TO LEAVE THE ROUGH WAY

9. The River and the Way parted for a time. They grew discouraged because the Way now was rough on their feet.
10. He grew discouraged over his discomfort; he wished for a better way; he saw what looked like a more pleasant way; he saw steps and walked up them to get a better look at that alternate way; he decided to compromise when he saw an easier parallel path; he overrode his brother's objections; and he finally led the way into Bypath Meadow.
11. After Jesus was baptized, the Holy Spirit descended on Him from heaven as a Dove. And the Father announced Christ's deity, as well as His own favor. Then, the Spirit led Him into the wilderness where He experienced temptation. He fought temptation with the strength of His resolve and by wielding Scripture against the devil.
12. (Your answer)

IN BY-PATH MEADOW

13. Vain-confidence. He fell into a pit and died there.
14. (Your answer)
15. We can darken our souls with a flood of guilt, regret, unworthiness, and abandonment when we gaze upon our past ingratitude, rebelliousness, and willfulness. This weakens our resolve and makes things seem bleaker.

SEIZED BY GIANT DESPAIR

16. Things got even worse when the Giant Despair found them sleeping, seized them, and locked them away in his "Dungeon of Despair." It seems they had confessed their sin but had not fully repented of all the entanglements. They only added to their misery by not fully dealing with their condition.

DISTRUST'S PERSUASIONS

17. Distrust. While Giant Despair metes out the afflictions, Distrust is the one with the big ideas for driving the pilgrims to self-destruction. Distrust is something that robs us of our confidence in God's compassionate grace and mercy. Once we believe God's grace has become unavailable to us, we are unreceptive to it and begin our descent into despair.

HOPEFUL REFUSES TO ABANDON ALL HOPE

18. A life with despair or death by suicide. Hopeful advises Christian that suicide is unlawful and not an option. Also, true to his name, he does not abandon hope. He thinks others may have escaped Giant Despair, or that the Giant may die, or forget to lock the gate. He also reminded Christian of his former bravery.
19. (Your answer)

REMEMBERING THE KEY OF PROMISE

20. This Key of Promise represents God's promises that were there all along.

ESCAPE FROM DOUBTING CASTLE

21. The pilgrims had been in a lengthy time of prayer.
22. (Your answer)
23. They helped others by building a monument to warn them.
24. (Your answer)

CHAPTER 12

TO BEGIN

(Your answer)

THE DELECTABLE MOUNTAINS

1. They were feeding their flocks. Faithful pastors must nurture those under their care. Jesus told Peter to feed and tend His lambs/sheep.
2. (Your answer)
3. They belong to Emmanuel, and He laid down His life for them. Pastors need to remember that the flock never belongs to them. They are simply under-shepherds. Peter instructs leaders to oversee the flock willingly and eagerly with pure motives. They should not domineer but be good examples. When Jesus (the Chief Shepherd) appears, they will receive a glorious crown.
4. a. *Knowledge*: A shepherd should study the Word and know it well, avoiding nonsense and focusing on the truth.
   b. *Experience*: Wisdom is learned by age. Church leaders should not be new believers/inexperienced, or they might fall into temptation.
   c. *Watchful:* Leaders must be very careful to watch both themselves and God's flock. Wolves will come among the flock to seduce them from the sheepfold, so leaders must stay alert.
   d. *Sincere:* True leaders will have sincere faith. They stick to scriptural truth. Their motive is love that comes from a pure heart, good conscience, and sincere faith. Also, they are motivated by sincere brotherly love.
5. Among other things, a leader must be hospitable. The Church must also be hospitable, entertaining strangers.

A MOUNTAIN CALLED ERROR

6. Paul advises Timothy to do his best for God, gaining God's approval by knowing the Scriptures and handling them properly. He wants Timothy to be a faithful shepherd, unlike the false shepherds Hymenacus and

Philetus. These two mishandled God's Word and promoted their own doctrine. This was dangerous to the Church.

7.   Many people were teaching false doctrines and leading entire households astray. Also, he foresaw an even more urgent time: A time when people would dismiss sound doctrine. A time when a proliferation of false teachers will lead them from the faith and into myths.

8.   (Your answer)

A MOUNTAIN CALLED CAUTION

9.   *Proverbs 21:16* That straying from the right way leads to dwelling in a graveyard with others who made that wrong choice. *Proverbs 13:20* That walking with wise companions brings wisdom, while walking with fools leads to harm. We should avoid following the Vain-confidences of this world.

10.   Blind guides, blind fools, blind men, blind Pharisees. They were dangerous because they were the blind leading the blind into a spiritual pit.

11.   Paul said that they had seen doctrinal truth about Jesus with their own eyes but that someone had bewitched them. Peter says to make every effort to grow in qualities like faith, virtue, knowledge, self-control, steadfastness, godliness, brotherly affection, and love. These will keep us from spiritual blindness and prevent a serious fall.

12.   (Your answer)

A BY-WAY TO HELL

13.   A warning like this is sure to keep the pilgrims sober and dependent on "the Strong One," always resisting hypocrisy in its many forms. Also, they must beware of hypocrites still ahead.

14.   He calls them serpents and vipers who are on their way to Hell. Jesus says to beware of the yeast of the Pharisees, which is hypocrisy. Be cautious, because yeast starts small and gradually spreads its influence until it affects the entire batch of dough.

15.   We must examine and test our lives to make sure we are truly in the faith. We must be disciplined in our walk with Christ, rooted and built up in Him, established in the faith, full of thanksgiving. We must be careful not let anyone rob us of a sound faith.

16.   (Your answer)

A VIEW OF THE CITY

17.   The hill's name is "Clear." They need a "perspective glass" to enable them to see through the earthly realm to the Celestial gates. Evidently lacking "skill," their hands shook.

18.   (Your answer)

19.   (Your answer)

20.   As leaders are true to their calling of carefully shepherding us, we should cooperate with them and have a submissive spirit. We don't want to make their lives miserable.

CHAPTER 13

TO BEGIN

(Your answer)

WALKING WITH IGNORANCE

1.   He neither understands nor values truth. In his puffed-up arrogance, he holds to a religion that suits him. It is easy, and it avoids the sacrifice of humbling himself before the Cross.

2.   Paul wants the Gentile believers to be humble about God's grace toward them. Ignorance of the truth breeds conceit, and he wants them always to remember the truth that God's grace alone saved them and that God still has a plan for the Jews.

3.   Both the Pharisee and Ignorance self-righteously trust in their own goodness before God. Because both are impressed with their good deeds, they believe God is equally impressed.

4.   (Your answer)

A MAN BEING CARRIED AWAY

5. Jesus warned that one who gets cleansed and then returns to his old life is like a person released from one demon only to be bound by many more. James warns not to let fleshly desires draw us into sin and death.

6. (Your answer)

THE STORY OF LITTLE-FAITH

7. Faint-heart, Mistrust, and Guilt. They took all his money.

8. Most likely present spiritual riches like confidence, comfort, liberty, peace, joy.

9. Rather than counting his blessings – that he still had his jewels (his soul going to heaven) – he constantly bemoaned his losses and let everyone know it.

10. Paul urges us to bear with each other, especially the strong with the weak. As Christ did, we should not live to please ourselves but others. It will take endurance and encouragement, but we should do our best to live harmoniously and glorify God together.

HOPEFUL MISJUDGES LITTLE-FAITH

11. He prays God's glorious riches upon us – the Spirit's power in our inner being, Christ's presence in our hearts by faith, His love rooted in us, our ability to know and experience its vastness – so that we will be filled with God. Also, he warns of our weakness lest we become over-confident.

12. (Your answer)

13. (Your answer)

14. Christian humbly recalls his own vulnerability. He well remembers his battle with Apollyon in the Valley of Humiliation. He moved on from there to the Valley of the Shadow of Death. He says he fought these three "journeyman thieves," and they were no small opponents. Even with his armor, Christian feels he barely escaped that onslaught from Hell.

15. These Scriptures advise us not to think too highly of ourselves. We should assess our lives realistically according to the measure of faith that God has given us. We should live harmoniously, walk humbly, associate with the lowly, and refrain from conceit. Humility precedes honor in the Christian life.

GREAT-GRACE AND FIGHTING THE GOOD FIGHT

16. The source of Great-grace's greatness is God's grace. He is a champion because he understands the power of grace. God's champions need to learn to rely on grace. Paul says that grace has made him the man he is. He testifies that he works really hard but that this, too, is a work of grace.

17. a. We should go out fully equipped with our armor, giving special attention to using our shield of faith. b. We should ask the King to send us out with a convoy to protect us, even the King Himself.

18. Christian wishes his battles were behind him but fears more await them ahead.

19. (Your answer)

CHAPTER 14

TO BEGIN

(Your answer)

THE PILGRIMS ARE DECEIVED

1. Another way joined their Way. Both went straight and seemed headed in the right direction, so they couldn't tell which to choose. Then a man in white steered them in the wrong direction.

2. Satan can make himself look like one of God's holy angels. Thus, it is not difficult for his servants to do so, too.

3. He is cunning and strategic, using great subtlety and craft to deceive.

4. Jesus knew the End Times would be dangerous. He urged them to be careful that no one would lead them astray.

5. They were abandoning the Lord and His grace for some other "Good News." He said that anyone preaching another Good News (which isn't really good news) is under a curse.

6. (Your answer)

ENCOUNTER WITH A SHINING ONE

7. A whip.
8. Of course, the first error would be that they became proud and careless. When the pilgrims got confused about the way to take, they forgot about their sheet of directions given for that purpose. They were careless when they trusted a flatterer's directions.
9. (Your answer)

MEETING ATHEIST

10. The Scripture warns us of scoffers who will mock the truth and obey their desires, not God's. But God is not mocked. There will be a day of reckoning for those who mock Him.
11. People like Atheist don't conduct an honest search. Their real issue is that they reject God to follow their own ungodly passions. They are worldly and devoid of the Holy Spirit. While they walk according to natural instincts, God's people walk by faith.
12. (Your answer)
13. That God reveals wonderful things to the "little children" of His Kingdom while keeping such treasures hidden from the wise of this world. Revealing the Father to His followers delights Him.

ON THE ENCHANTED GROUND

14. This is a dangerous spiritual attack that causes spiritual sleepiness.
15. (Your answer)
16. a. We must remain earnest in our pilgrimage so we will hold on to our hope to the end. We cannot afford sluggishness. Rather, we should be as those who persevere in faith to inherit the promises. b. There are consequences for sleeping, so we must guard ourselves against sleepiness. We want be alert and ready for Jesus when He returns.
17. This Scripture implies that they are being overtaken by spiritual deadness. It demands that they wake up; and promises that, as they do, Christ will shine on them.
18. (Your answer)
19. (Your answer)

CHAPTER 15

TO BEGIN

(Your answer)

HOPEFUL TELLS HIS STORY

1. (Your answer)
2. (Your answer)
3. The things that are seen represent the earthly/transient realm (seen by physical eyes). The things that are unseen represent the heavenly/eternal realm (seen through eyes of faith).
4. (Your answer)
5. (Your answer)
6. We can learn a lot from Paul: To request prayer for the right words to explain God's plan of salvation boldly, to request prayer that we won't falter in our commitment in this, to commit ourselves never to shrink from telling people the truth they need to hear, and to maintain an earnest desire to finish our assignment well.
7. 1. He didn't realize that God was acting on him. 2. He loved sin. 3. His old friends were important to him, and he didn't want to lose them. 4. He felt such intense conviction that he tried not to think about it.
8. That He would convict people of their sin, God's righteousness, and the coming judgment.

ATTEMPTED REFORMS AND RENEWED CONVICTION

9. Hopeful tried to reform himself. He tried to be good and also rid himself of his sinful friends. He did all kinds of religious duties.

10. Unfortunately, we cannot redeem ourselves. We may try to be good, but our righteousness is impure and polluted. In ourselves, we are still doomed.

11. Salvation comes by grace by responding in faith. It is God's gift, not a result of works. If we could work our way into salvation, we would try to grab the credit. God wants us to do good, but good works should be our response to grace.

THE DEBT AND POWER OF SIN

12. First, Hopeful might pay off his current debt of sin, but he still owes an enormous debt accumulated from his former sins. Second, even if he were previously guiltless, he daily would accumulate enough guilt to land him in Hell.

13. (Your answer)

A SAVIOR IS NEEDED

14. Hopeful had watched and listened to Faithful. Because of Faithful's wise "seasoning," Hopeful was hungry to know more and felt safe in coming to Faithful.

15. That Jesus Christ is the Mighty God. He sits at the Most High God's right hand. Upon the earth, He lived, died, and resurrected for us. He sacrificed Himself, which was enough to pay our debt.

AN INVITATION EXTENDED

16. Faithful directs Hopeful to Christ to see for himself. Similarly, Philip directs Nathaniel to come and see Christ for himself.

17. Faithful sends Hopeful to God's Word. Paul says that the Scriptures give wisdom to receive salvation by faith in Jesus Christ.

18. Faithful calls Christ's throne a mercy seat. Jesus depicts His throne as a seat that metes out both eternal judgment and mercy.

19. This prayer humbly acknowledges the guilt of personal sin, asks for faith to believe, appeals to God for mercy, affirms that Christ is the only hope of salvation, requests salvation, and calls on God to glorify Himself through this work of grace.

HE RECEIVES A REVELATION

20. He didn't need to be righteous for God to accept him. He looked to Jesus alone to grant righteousness and settle his debt of sin. Jesus took the penalty by shedding His blood, and Hopeful simply needed to accept salvation gratefully.

21. He overflowed with love for the Name, the people, and the ways of Jesus. He felt ashamed of his former life that ignored Christ's "glorious beauty." He loved holiness and wanted to live for Christ's glory. He would have died for Him.

22. As time goes on, we can get spiritually sluggish. When we see this happening in ourselves and in each other, we need to pull together, encourage each other. We should think of ways to stir up and awaken our flagging spirits to fervent love and good works.

23. (Your answer)

CHAPTER 16

TO BEGIN

(Your answer)

THE PILGRIMS DISCUSS JUSTIFICATION WITH IGNORANCE

1. The two mature pilgrims make Ignorance uncomfortable. Their allegiance to the truth meddles with his convictions.

2. (Your answer)

3. Two people can help each other when they stumble. We are called to help restore each other. We rely on each other—confessing our sins, praying for each other, and even bringing spiritual restoration.

4. The faith Ignorance describes seems to rest in wishful mental exercises. Paul, on the other hand, describes wrestling with the soul's intrinsic evil. Human effort cannot overcome this powerful internal "law." It requires a Deliverer – Jesus Christ.

5. Jesus says that to be His disciple, we must renounce what is ours. Peter said that the other disciples and he had left everything to follow Jesus.

6. Our hearts are unreliable and can deceive us. The Lord, however, sees what's in our hearts and minds, and He will judge us accordingly.

7. Good thoughts about ourselves should agree with God's Word. God's Word says that in ourselves we are unrighteous. If we humble ourselves and agree with God's Word about our ways, our thoughts are good. Ignorance disagrees. Because God's Word contradicts his beliefs about himself, he rejects its claims.

8. (Your answer)

9. A right view of God acknowledges that He knows us better than we know ourselves. Indeed, we can hide nothing from Him. Also, He has no tolerance for self-righteousness.

10. He believes either God will accept him because of his successful obedience or somehow Christ will make his efforts acceptable to God. In effect, he gets part of the credit for his salvation. In reality, Christ alone won our salvation.

11. (Your answer)

12. Ignorance's faith is: a. Imaginary (because it is found nowhere in God's Word); b. False (because a person justifies himself); c. Deceitful (because a person is justified by his own good actions). d. Consequence: God's wrath on Judgment Day.

13. God's righteous Law makes us aware of our lost condition. By faith, we flee to Christ's righteousness. We realize His obedience--not our own good efforts--makes us acceptable by His grace.

14. (Your answer)

15. *Matthew 11:25-26* The Father revealed hidden truth to "little children." *Ephesians 1:15-21* He prays that God will give us a spirit of wisdom and revelation. *Proverbs 29:18* Where there is no revelation, people cast off restraint. (They run amok to their undoing.)

16. Yes, the Bible does address this and states clearly that we must not deceive ourselves.

THEY DISCUSS GODLY FEAR

17. (Your answer)

18. Godly fear convicts us of sin; it drives us to Christ for salvation; it gives us a deep reverence for God, His Word, and His ways that prevents our turning from Him; it keeps us from doing anything that might dishonor God, interrupt our relationship with Him, or grieve His Spirit.

19. To be saved, people must call on the Lord. But they can't do that unless they believe in Him, and they can't believe in Him unless someone shares the Gospel with them. Those who heed the Spirit's call to evangelize have beautiful feet.

THEY DISCUSS BACKSLIDING

20. This would be a tendency toward any self-centered approach that turns people from godly fear, convincing them to save themselves through their own good efforts or works.

21. a. There was an awakening to sin and the prospect of Hell. The feelings pass, however, and the person returns to his former ways. b. For fear of man and what godliness might cost, the person falls back in step with the world. c. Pride prevents them from enduring the contempt that often accompanies a sincere Christian pilgrimage. d. Facing their guilt and the fear of Hell seems too much to bear. Rather than fleeing to Christ, they hide from their spiritual condition and harden their hearts.

22. a. Avoiding thoughts of God, death, and judgment b. Casting off personal obligations like prayer, purity, watchfulness, repentance c. Rejecting friendships with dedicated Christians d. Growing indifferent to public obligations like church attendance. e. Faultfinding as an excuse to reject the faith. f. Running with the wrong crowd. g. Giving in to secret sins h. Returning to a former lost and hopeless state.

23. (Your answer)

CHAPTER 17

TO BEGIN

(Your answer)

Enjoying the Country of Beulah

1. Scripture portrays Christ as the Bridegroom and the Church as His cherished bride. We currently ready ourselves for the "marriage supper" being prepared for us.
2. (Your answer)
3. We begin our pilgrimage with a measure of God's strength. Despite our human frailties, we move forward and increasingly grow in strength until reaching our destination.
4. (Your answer)
5. Loud voices proclaiming God's promises.
6. They see the City and become lovesick with intense longing.
7. Paul's amazing heavenly experience convinced him that dying was gain. Yet he lived for Christ and knew he had more work to do in helping the believers to progress in their faith.
8. (Your answer)

Two Shining Ones

9. (Your answer)

The Unavoidable River

10. It is a very deep River that they must cross without the aid of the Shining Ones and without the benefit of a bridge. It will take faith alone to cross.
11. It represents death. Thinking about dying and going to heaven can be quite different than actually going through the process.
12. He testified that he had fought the good fight, finished his course, and kept the faith. The Lord had a crown of righteousness to give him and also one to give everyone who looks forward to seeing Him.
13. Enoch and Elijah. God took Enoch away. He simply disappeared. Elijah rode a flaming chariot to heaven in a whirlwind.
14. This will happen when Christ returns at His Second Coming. Those alive, along with those who have died, will immediately be caught up to meet Christ in the air and be with Him forever.
15. It depends on the faith of each individual Christian who must cross it.

Passing through the River

16. (Your answer)
17. Hope will never disappoint us.

On the Other Side

18. The Shining Ones helped them. Also, they got to leave their encumbering mortal garments behind in the River.

What the Pilgrims Can Expect Ahead

19. There will be multitudes of joyful angels in the City; along with the spirits of God's people, now perfect. They will see paradise; eat from the fruit of the Tree of Life; receive white robes; enjoy fellowship with their King for all eternity; experience no more sorrow, affliction, or death; and meet the great biblical heroes.
20. They must receive consolation and joy for their former troubles; reap what they have sown in their prayers, tears and suffering for the King; receive treasures; wear crowns of gold; experience perpetual joy as they see their king as He truly is; serve Him continually with jubilation; delight at seeing and hearing Him; enjoy friends and loved ones who are there; and know the joy of receiving everyone who follows. They will be clothed with glory and majesty, and suitably equipped to ride out with the King of Glory when the trumpet

sounds and He rides out on the clouds. They must, as well, sit beside Him and participate in the judgment on His and our enemies; return with Him when He returns to the City; and dwell with Him there forever.

A Glad Procession to the Gate

21. (Your answer)

They Gain Entrance to the City

22. This is their proof of salvation, their title to heaven.
23. They are singing loudly along with multitudes of others, "To Him who sits on the throne and to the Lamb be praise and honor and glory and power forever and ever!"

Final Outcome of Ignorance

24. He ends it with Ignorance being taken to Hell. Ignorance avoided the Cross and entered the Way illegitimately. The whole way, he stubbornly held to his own proud doctrine. Vain-hope got him across the River, but that was all. Despite his misguided confidence, he had no certificate with which to gain admittance.
25. (Your answer)

In Closing

26. (Your answer)

MEMORY VERSES

Chapter 1
Blessed are those whose strength is in you, who have set their hearts on pilgrimage. -- Psalm 84:5

Chapter 2
Be careful that you don't let anyone rob you through his philosophy and vain deceit, after the tradition of men, after the elements of the world, and not after Christ. -- Colossians 2:8

Chapter 3
Teach me to do your will, for you are my God. Your Spirit is good. Lead me in the land of uprightness. -- Psalm 143:10

Chapter 4
For the word of the cross is folly to those who are perishing, but to us who are being saved it is the power of God. -- 1 Corinthians 1:18

Chapter 5
Let's consider how to provoke one another to love and good works, not forsaking our own assembling together, as the custom of some is, but exhorting one another, and so much the more, as you see the Day approaching. -- Hebrews 10:25

Chapter 6
For though we walk in the flesh, we are not waging war according to the flesh. For the weapons of our warfare are not of the flesh but have divine power to destroy strongholds. -- 2 Corinthians 10:3-4

Chapter 7
No temptation has taken you except what is common to man. God is faithful, who will not allow you to be tempted above what you are able, but will with the temptation also make the way of escape, that you may be able to endure it. --1 Corinthians 10:13

Chapter 8
For our gospel did not come to you in word only, but also in power, and in the Holy Spirit and in much assurance, as you know what kind of men we were among you for your sake. -- 1 Thessalonians 1:5 NKJV

Chapter 9
I am coming quickly! Hold firmly that which you have, so that no one takes your crown. -- Revelation 3:11
Yes, and all who desire to live godly in Christ Jesus will suffer persecution. -- 2 Timothy 3:12

Chapter 10
Don't love the world or the things that are in the world. If anyone loves the world, the Father's love isn't in him. -- 1 John 2:15

Chapter 11

But I will hope continually and will praise you yet more and more. My mouth will tell of your righteous acts, of your deeds of salvation all the day, for their number is past my knowledge. -- Psalm 71:14-15

Chapter 12

But we beg you, brothers, to know those who labor among you, and are over you in the Lord, and admonish you, and to respect and honor them in love for their work's sake. Be at peace among yourselves. -- 1 Thessalonians 5:12-13

Chapter 13

But you, beloved, keep building up yourselves on your most holy faith, praying in the Holy Spirit. Keep yourselves in God's love, looking for the mercy of our Lord Jesus Christ to eternal life. --Jude 1:20-21

Chapter 14

Trust in the LORD with all your heart, and do not lean on your own understanding. 6 In all your ways acknowledge him, and he will make straight your paths. 7 Be not wise in your own eyes; fear the LORD, and turn away from evil. -- Proverbs 3:5-7

Chapter 15

For there is only one God and one Mediator who can reconcile God and humanity — the man Christ Jesus. He gave his life to purchase freedom for everyone. This is the message God gave to the world at just the right time. -- 1 Timothy 2:5-6

Chapter 16

Fear of the LORD is the foundation of wisdom. Knowledge of the Holy One results in good judgment. -- Proverbs 9:10 NLT

Chapter 17

No eye has seen, no ear has heard, and no mind has imagined what God has prepared for those who love him. -- 1 Corinthians 2:9 NLT

DAILY STUDY PLAN OPTIONS

8 Week/40 Day Plan: Chapters 1-2, 3-4, 5-6, 7-8, 9-10, 11-13 (Q 1-12), 13 (Q 13-18), 14-15*
9 Week Plan: Chapters 1-2, 3-4, 5-6, 7-8, 9-10, 11-12, 13-14, 15-16, 17 *
12 Week Plan: Chapters 1-2, 3-4, 5-6, 7-8, 9, 10-11, 12, 13-14, 15, 16, 17*
17 Week Plan: Chapters 1, 2, 3, 4, 5, 6, 7, 8, 9, 10, 11, 12, 13, 14, 15, 16, 17 *
*Add extra meeting for the optional Celebration Meeting

8 Week Plan

Week one (Ch. 1-2)	**Week three (Ch. 5-6)**	**Week five (Ch. 9-10)**	**Week seven (Ch. 13 Q 13-19; 14-15)**
Day 1. Ch. 1, Q 1-7	Day 1. Ch. 5, Q 1-9	Day 1. Ch. 9, Q 1-9	Day 1. Ch. 13, Q 11-19
Day 2. Ch. 1, Q 8-15	Day 2. Ch. 5, Q 10-18	Day 2. Ch. 9, Q 10-21	Day 2. Ch. 14, Q 1-9
Day 3. Ch. 1, Q 16-22	Day 3. Ch. 6, Q 1-5	Day 3. Ch. 10, Q 1-7	Day 3. Ch. 14, Q 10-19
Day 4. Ch. 2, Q 1-10	Day 4. Ch. 6, Q 6-14	Day 4. Ch. 10, Q 8-16	Day 4. Ch. 15, Q 1-13
Day 5. Ch. 2, Q 11-19	Day 5. Ch. 6, Q 15-25	Day 5. Ch. 10, Q 17-21	Day 5. Ch. 15, Q 14-23
Week two (Ch. 3-4)	**Week four (Ch. 7-8)**	**Week six (Ch. 11-13 Q 1-12)**	**Week eight (Ch. 16-17)**
Day 1. Ch. 3, Q 1-9	Day 1. Ch. 7, Q 1-6	Day 1. Ch. 11, Q 1-12	Day 1. Ch. 16, Q 1-10
Day 2. Ch. 3, Q 10-21	Day 2. Ch. 7, Q 7-9	Day 2. Ch. 11, Q 13-24	Day 2. Ch. 16, Q 11-16
Day 3. Ch. 4, Q 1-6	Day 3. Ch. 7, Q 10-14	Day 3. Ch. 12, Q 1-12	Day 3. Ch. 16, Q 17-23
Day 4. Ch. 4, Q 7-13	Day 4. Ch. 8, Q 1-10	Day 4. Ch. 12, Q 13-20	Day 4. Ch. 17, Q 1-15
Day 5. Ch. 4, Q 14-20	Day 5. Ch. 8, Q 11-22	Day 5. Ch. 13, Q 1-10	Day 5. Ch. 17, Q 16-25

9 Week Plan

Week one (Ch. 1-2)
Day 1. Ch. 1, Q 1-7
Day 2. Ch. 1, Q 8-15
Day 3. Ch. 1, Q 16-22
Day 4. Ch. 2, Q 1-10
Day 5. Ch. 2, Q 11-19

Week two (Ch. 3-4)
Day 1. Ch. 3, Q 1-9
Day 2. Ch. 3, Q 10-21
Day 3. Ch. 4, Q 1-6
Day 4. Ch. 4, Q 7-13
Day 5. Ch. 4, Q 14-20

Week three (Ch. 5-6)
Day 1. Ch. 5, Q 1-9
Day 2. Ch. 5, Q 10-18
Day 3. Ch. 6, Q 1-5
Day 4. Ch. 6, Q 6-14
Day 5. Ch. 6, Q 15-25

Week four (Ch. 7-8)
Day 1. Ch. 7, Q 1-6
Day 2. Ch. 7, Q 7-9
Day 3. Ch. 7, Q 10-14
Day 4. Ch. 8, Q 1-10
Day 5. Ch. 8, Q 11-22

Week five (Ch. 9-10)
Day 1. Ch. 9, Q 1-9
Day 2. Ch. 9, Q 10-21
Day 3. Ch. 10, Q 1-7
Day 4. Ch. 10, Q 8-16
Day 5. Ch. 10, Q 17-21

Week six (Ch. 11-12)
Day 1. Ch. 11, Q 1-12
Day 2. Ch. 11, Q 13-24
Day 3. Ch. 12, Q 1-5
Day 4. Ch. 12, Q 6-12
Day 5. Ch. 12, Q 13-20

Week seven (Ch. 13-14)
Day 1. Ch. 13 1Q 1-6
Day 2. Ch. 13, Q 7-15
Day 3. Ch. 13, Q 16-19
Day 4. Ch. 14, Q 1-9
Day 5. Ch. 14, Q 10-19

Week eight (Ch. 15-16)
Day 1. Ch.15, Q 1-13
Day 2. Ch.15, Q 14-23
Day 3. Ch.16, Q 1-8
Day 4. Ch.16, Q 9-16
Day 5. Ch.16, Q 17-23

Week nine (Ch. 17)
Day 1. Ch. 17, Q 1-8
Day 2. Ch. 17, Q 9-15
Day 3. Ch. 17, Q 16-18
Day 4. Ch. 17, Q 19-21
Day 5. Ch. 17, Q 22-25

12 Week Plan

Week one (Ch. 1-2)
Day 1. Ch. 1, Q 1-7
Day 2. Ch. 1, Q 8-15
Day 3. Ch. 1, Q 16-22
Day 4. Ch. 2, Q 1-10
Day 5. Ch. 2, Q 11-19

Week two (Ch. 3-4)
Day 1. Ch. 3, Q 1-9
Day 2. Ch. 3, Q 10-21
Day 3. Ch. 4, Q 1-6
Day 4. Ch. 4, Q 7-13
Day 5. Ch. 4, Q 14-20

Week three (Ch. 5-6)
Day 1. Ch. 5, Q 1-9
Day 2. Ch. 5, Q 10-18
Day 3. Ch. 6, Q 1-5
Day 4. Ch. 6, Q 6-14
Day 5. Ch. 6, Q 15-25

Week four (Ch. 7)
Day 1. Ch. 7, Q 1-4
Day 2. Ch. 7, Q 5-6
Day 3. Ch. 7, Q 7-8
Day 4. Ch. 7, Q 9-10
Day 5. Ch. 7, Q 11-14

Week five (Ch. 8)
Day 1. Ch. 8, Q 1-5
Day 2. Ch. 8, Q 6-9
Day 3. Ch. 8, Q 10-14
Day 4. Ch. 8, Q 15-18
Day 5. Ch. 8, Q 19-22

Week six (Ch. 9)
Day 1. Ch. 9, Q 1-5
Day 2. Ch. 9, Q 6-9
Day 3. Ch. 9, Q 10-13
Day 4. Ch. 9, Q 14-18
Day 5. Ch. 9, Q 19-21

Week seven (Ch. 10-11)
Day 1. Ch. 10, Q 1-7
Day 2. Ch. 10, Q 8-16
Day 3. Ch. 10, Q 17-21
Day 4. Ch. 11, Q 1-12
Day 5. Ch. 11, Q 13-24

Week eight (Ch. 12)
Day 1. Ch. 12, Q 1-4
Day 2. Ch. 12, Q 5-8
Day 3. Ch. 12, Q 9-12
Day 4. Ch. 12, Q 13-16
Day 5. Ch 12, Q 17-20

Week nine (Ch. 13-14)
Day 1. Ch. 13, Q 1-6
Day 2. Ch. 13, Q 7-15
Day 3. Ch. 13, Q 16-19
Day 4. Ch. 14, Q 1-9
Day 5. Ch. 14, Q 10-19

Week ten (Ch. 15)
Day 1. Ch. 15, Q 1-6
Day 2. Ch. 15, Q 7-11
Day 3. Ch. 15, Q 12-15
Day 3. Ch. 15, Q 16-19
Day 3. Ch. 15, Q 20-23

Week eleven (Ch. 16)
Day 1. Ch.16, Q 1-6
Day 2. Ch.16, Q 7-11
Day 3. Ch.16, Q 12-16
Day 4. Ch.16, Q 17-19
Day 5. Ch.16, Q 20-23

Week twelve (Ch. 17)
Day 1. Ch. 17, Q 1-8
Day 2. Ch. 17, Q 9-15
Day 3. Ch. 17, Q 16-18
Day 4. Ch. 17, Q 19-21
Day 5. Ch. 17, Q 22-25

17 Week Plan

Week one (Ch. 1)
Day 1. Ch. 1, Q 1-5
Day 2. Ch. 1, Q 6-9
Day 3. Ch. 1, Q 10-14
Day 4. Ch. 17, Q 15-17
Day 5. Ch. 17, Q 18-22

Week two (Ch. 2)
Day 1. Ch. 2, Q 1-5
Day 2. Ch. 2, Q 6-10
Day 3. Ch. 2, Q 11-14
Day 4. Ch. 2, Q 15-17
Day 5. Ch. 2, Q 18-19

Week three (Ch. 3)
Day 1. Ch. 3, Q 1-5
Day 2. Ch. 3, Q 6-9
Day 3. Ch. 3, Q 10-13
Day 4. Ch. 3, Q 14-16
Day 5. Ch. 3, Q 17-21

Week four (Ch. 4)
Day 1. Ch. 4, Q 1-6
Day 2. Ch. 4, Q 7-10
Day 3. Ch. 4, Q 11-13
Day 4. Ch. 4, Q 14-17
Day 5. Ch. 4, Q 18-20

Week five (Ch. 5)
Day 1. Ch. 5, Q 1-4
Day 2. Ch. 5, Q 5-9
Day 3. Ch. 5, Q 10-12
Day 4. Ch. 5, Q 13-15
Day 5. Ch. 5, Q 16-18

Week six (Ch. 6)
Day 1. Ch. 6, Q 1-5
Day 2. Ch. 6, Q 6-9
Day 3. Ch. 6, Q 10-14
Day 4. Ch. 6, Q 15-19
Day 5. Ch. 6, Q 20-25

Week seven (Ch. 7)
Day 1. Ch. 7, Q 1-4
Day 2. Ch. 7, Q 5-6
Day 3. Ch. 7, Q 7-8
Day 4. Ch. 7, Q 9-10
Day 5. Ch. 7, Q 11-14

Week eight (Ch. 8)
Day 1. Ch. 8, Q 1-5
Day 2. Ch. 8, Q 6-9
Day 3. Ch. 8, Q 10-14
Day 4. Ch. 8, Q 15-18
Day 5. Ch. 8, Q 19-22

Week nine (Ch. 9)
Day 1. Ch. 9, Q 1-5
Day 2. Ch. 9, Q 6-9
Day 3. Ch. 9, Q 10-13
Day 4. Ch. 9, Q 14-18
Day 5. Ch. 9, Q 19-21

Week ten (Ch. 10)
Day 1. Ch. 10, Q 1-5
Day 2. Ch. 10, Q 6-9
Day 3. Ch. 10, Q 10-12
Day 4. Ch. 10, Q 13-16
Day 5. Ch. 10, Q 17-21

Week eleven (Ch. 11)
Day 1. Ch. 11, Q 1-5
Day 2. Ch. 11, Q 6-8
Day 3. Ch. 12, Q 9-15
Day 4. Ch. 12, Q 16-19
Day 5. Ch. 12, Q 20-24

Week twelve (Ch. 12)
Day 1. Ch. 12, Q 1-4
Day 2. Ch. 12, Q 5-8
Day 3. Ch. 12, Q 9-12
Day 4. Ch. 12, Q 13-16
Day 5. Ch 12, Q 17-20

Week thirteen (Ch. 13)
Day 1. Ch. 13, Q 1-6
Day 2. Ch. 13, Q 7-10
Day 3. Ch. 13, Q 11-14
Day 4. Ch. 13, Q 13-15
Day 5. Ch 13, Q 16-19

Week fourteen (Ch. 14)
Day 1. Ch. 14, Q 1-6
Day 2. Ch. 14, Q 7-9
Day 3. Ch. 14, Q 10-13
Day 4. Ch. 14, Q 14-16
Day 5. Ch. 14, Q 1

Week fifteen (Ch. 15)
Day 1. Ch. 15, Q 1-6
Day 2. Ch. 15, Q 7-11
Day 3. Ch. 15, Q 12-15
Day 3. Ch. 15, Q 16-19
Day 3. Ch. 15, Q 20-23

Week sixteen (Ch. 16)
Day 1. Ch.16, Q 1-6
Day 2. Ch.16, Q 7-11
Day 3. Ch.16, Q 12-16
Day 4. Ch.16, Q 17-19
Day 5. Ch.16, Q 20-23

Week seventeen (Ch. 17)
Day 1. Ch. 17, Q 1-8
Day 2. Ch. 17, Q 9-15
Day 3. Ch. 17, Q 16-18
Day 4. Ch. 17, Q 19-21
Day 5. Ch. 17, Q 22-25

RELATED RESOURCES FROM CHERYL FORD

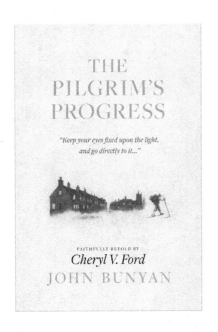

The Pilgrim's Progress

Cheryl's award-winning book now beautifully repackaged in this new edition, released November 2016.

The Pilgrim's Progress Devotional

A book packed with 365 days of inspiration and deep insights for the Christian pilgrimage.

Look for my books at www.CherylFord.com and where books are sold.

Printed in the United States
By Bookmasters